KU-496-250

Contents

KEY TO MAPS

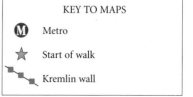

Ⓜ Metro

★ Start of walk

▪▪ Kremlin wall

Introduction

Russia – few do not sense a frisson of anticipation at the mere mention of the word. The mind conjures with images of haunting natural beauty and exotic architecture, imperial extravagance and bleak communist uniformity, inspired arts, simple-hearted *joie de vivre* and chilling despotism; the land seems so familiar yet remains, at heart, a mystery.

Typical Russian skyline

It is a mystery which even the Russians themselves do not claim to have fathomed, but its depths and paradoxes cannot be better revealed to the foreign visitor than through the two great cities of Moscow (*Moskva*) and St Petersburg (*Sankt Peterburg*).

In the 1980s, both cities were at the forefront of a battle to overcome the consequences of more than 70 years of communist rule, as Mikhail Gorbachev's twin policies of perestroika and glasnost took root, plunging the nation into the throes of reforms whose outcome is still far from guaranteed. Both cities emerged bloody but unbowed from the turbulent 1990s to witness the advent of President Vladimir Putin. Russia is open as never before to foreign tourism. Visitors to Moscow and St Petersburg now have the enviable opportunity to witness Russia's great democratic experiment as it faces the challenges of the new millennium.

Palace Square, St Petersburg

MOSCOW & ST PETERSBURG

BY

CHRIS BOOTH

Produced by

Thomas Cook Publishing

Written by Chris Booth
Updated by Christopher and Melanie Rice
Original photography by Ken Paterson and Jon Arnold
Updated photography by Demetrio Carrasco
Original design by Laburnum Technologies Pvt Ltd

Editing and page layout by Cambridge Publishing
Management Ltd, Unit 2, Burr Elm Court, Caldecote CB3 7NU
Series Editor: Karen Beaulah

Published by Thomas Cook Publishing
A division of Thomas Cook Tour Operations Ltd

PO Box 227, The Thomas Cook Business Park,
Units 15–16, Coningsby Road, Peterborough PE3 8SB, United Kingdom
E-mail: books@thomascook.com
www.thomascookpublishing.com
Tel: +44 (0) 1733 416477

ISBN-13: 978-1-84157-570-4
ISBN-10: 1-84157-570-4

Text © 2006 Thomas Cook Publishing
Maps © 2006 Thomas Cook Publishing
Moscow and St Petersburg metro maps © Communication Ltd
First edition © 2004 Thomas Cook Publishing
Second edition © 2006 Thomas Cook Publishing

Project Editor: Linda Bass
Production/DTP Editor: Steven Collins

All rights reserved. No part of this publication may be reproduced, stored in a retrieval system
or transmitted, in any form or by any means, electronic, mechanical, recording or otherwise,
in any part of the world, without prior permission of the publisher. Requests for permission
should be addressed to Thomas Cook Publishing, PO Box 227, The Thomas Cook Business
Park, Units 15–16, Coningsby Road, Peterborough PE3 8SB, United Kingdom.

Although every care has been taken in compiling this publication, and the contents are
believed to be correct at the time of printing, Thomas Cook Tour Operations Ltd cannot
accept any responsibility for errors or omissions, however caused, or for changes in details
given in the guidebook, or for the consequences of any reliance on the information provided.

The opinions and assessments expressed in this book do not necessarily represent those of
Thomas Cook Tour Operations Ltd.

Printed and bound in Spain by: Grafo Industrias Gráficas, Basauri.

Cover design by: Liz Lyons Design, Oxford.
Front cover credits: Left © Harald Sund/Getty; centre © Peter Titmuss/Alamy; right © Bruno
Morandi/Alamy
Back cover credits: Left © Jonathan Smith/Alamy; right © Pieter Estersohn/Getty

The former might and glory of the Soviet Union represented in this statue

'If ever your sons should be discontented with France, try my receipt,' wrote the Marquis de Custine after a visit in the 19th century. 'Tell them to go to Russia. It is a useful journey for every foreigner: who has well examined that country will be content to live anywhere else.' The sentiment was to be echoed for another hundred years and more in travellers' tales of morose shopkeepers, police informers, inedible food and bloody-minded bureaucrats.

Though these ghosts of Russia's past have still to be fully exorcised, Moscow and St Petersburg today have so much more to recommend them. As well as the treasures of art and architecture, both cities are ablaze with an infectious, creative vitality that means a first trip to Russia will rarely be the last. To meet first hand a people who were once forbidden to fraternise with westerners and whom westerners once feared is an unforgettable experience. And as travel becomes ever easier, the warmth and overwhelming hospitality of the Russians is the impression likely to last longest. Whatever the labyrinthine mysteries of the country, it will not disappoint.

A foreign visitor to Russia will experience a unique atmosphere that can be found nowhere else. Russia has its own life philosophy based on a mixture of past hardships and the relative freedom of today. It is a philosophy that to strangers may seem one full of irony and black humour.

Russian Federation

FINLAND
ESTONIA ■ St Petersburg
LATVIA
THUANIA ■ Moscow
BELARUS
UKRAINE

RUSSIA

KAZAKHSTAN

MONGOLIA

CHINA

Okhotniy Ryad, a favourite venue for walks and shopping, located right next to the Moscow Kremlin

Geography

Situated close to Russia's western frontier, St Petersburg was once the hub of a vast empire reaching 9,500km (5,900 miles) eastwards from the Baltic coast to the Pacific Ocean and almost 5,000km (3,105 miles) from the Arctic to the Caspian Sea. Today the successor to that empire, the Russian Federation, still extends over a staggering nine time zones of Russian territory. Its capital is Moscow.

A typical Moscow building standing guard

The Basics

Built on the important Moskva River, Moscow was ideally placed to dominate trade among the Russian princedoms. It never looked back. With a population of almost ten million, Moscow is today the world's sixth-largest city and the focus of the aspirations of most of Russia's other 143 million citizens.

St Petersburg is the most northerly of the world's big cities and its five million inhabitants share the same latitude with those of Anchorage in Alaska. Its 44 islands are in the Neva delta on the Gulf of Finland, making for a damp and windy climate. Summer evenings are long, especially the White Nights from 25 May to 16 July. The longest 'day' (around 21 June) actually lasts for 18,453 minutes!

As Hitler and Napoleon discovered, winter can be formidably cold, as low as −42°C (−44°F) in Moscow. 'Russia has two generals in which she can trust,' Nicholas I remarked, 'Generals Janvier and Février.'

While both cities churn out machine tools, vehicles and chemicals, ever more people are turning to the once despised profession of 'biznesmyen', trading whatever comes their way and satisfying a nation long starved of consumer goods.

The Economics of Reform

Economics rather than politics spelled the end for the communist system. A series of Five Year Plans had huge success in turning the USSR into an industrial giant. But growth of six per cent a year had collapsed to negative figures by the mid-1980s. Harvests rotted in the fields and life was characterised by the saying: 'We pretend to work and they pretend to pay us.'

In the end, the October Revolution proved no match for the information revolution. Herculean tractor production figures were meaningless in a world dominated by computers: in 1987, the USSR possessed just 100,000 personal computers compared with US annual production of over five million! Something had to change.

The Cost of Communism

Following Stalin's declaration that 'there are no fortresses that communism cannot storm', Soviet planners in quest of ever-higher economic targets wreaked havoc with the environment. A scheme to reverse the flow of Siberia's rivers was narrowly avoided, but the country is scarred by other ecological disasters.

Pollution in some industrial towns is so high that children need regular doses of pure oxygen. Lake Baikal, containing a fifth of the world's fresh water, is damaged by waste from the cellulose plants on its shores. Parts of western Russia were severely affected by radiation from the nuclear reactor fire at Chernobyl in 1986. Both Moscow and St Petersburg are periodically rocked by rumours about the emissions of their many secret factories.

Pollution combined with poor diet and hard work accounts for people's low life expectancy – 59 for men and 73 for women.

Mighty Russia

For all the pain of reform, Russia's natural and human wealth is unrivalled. Massive reserves of oil, coal and natural gas remain to be tapped, attracting western investors to the Siberian permafrost, while the Ural Mountains comprise 2,000km (1,240 miles) of rich mineral deposits. Timber resources are similarly assured – well over half the country is densely forested. What's more, the population is highly educated; the USSR boasted nearly 15 million active scientists and engineers.

This vast cohort of engineers and technicians ensures that Russian technology, backed by vast resources, is slowly reaching its once lost fame. Medical breakthroughs and high-tech military and aviation improvements are regularly made public. They are not improvements merely stated on paper, as was often the case in the past, but they are real, tangible improvements.

The Moskva River, viewed from the Kalinin Bridge

History

988	Prince Vladimir, ruler of the Russian state in Kiev, converts to Christianity.
1147	Yuri Dolgorukiy (Long Arm) establishes Moscow at the confluence of the Moskva and Neglinnaya rivers. Moscow becomes capital of the Principality of Muscovy.
1237	Khan Batu of the Golden Horde sacks Moscow. Tartar domination is to last for two-and-a-half centuries.
1453	The fall of Constantinople. Moscow henceforth is referred to as the 'Third and Last Rome'. The Byzantine double-headed eagle becomes the emblem of state.
1584	Ivan IV ('the Terrible') dies. Brutal regimentation of a poor land and people has made Muscovy a formidable European power.
1613	Mikhail Romanov is elected Tsar of all the Russias; his dynasty will last till 1917.
1682	Peter the Great's accession to the throne aged ten.
1703	Peter the Great founds St Petersburg on 16 May.
1712	Moscow razed by fire. St Petersburg is proclaimed the new capital.
1789	The French Revolution quashes Catherine the Great's experiment with liberalism.
1812	Napoleon invades Russia. Muscovites burn their city to drive out the invaders.
1825	Decembrists' revolt, led by educated officers later banished or executed.
1854	The Crimean War lays bare the backwardness of Russian society.
1861	Alexander II's decree abolishing serfdom.
1881	Alexander II is assassinated by terrorists belonging to the revolutionary People's Will movement.
1894	Nicholas II ascends the throne.
1905	Revolutionary disturbances throughout Russia result in

introduction of
a constitution and
an elected assembly
(Duma).

1917 The February Revolution
leads to the abdication
of Nicholas II. A
provisional government
is in power till the
Bolshevik putsch on
25 October. On
16 November Moscow
is restored as capital.

1918 The tsar and his family
are executed. Civil war
and foreign intervention
last till 1921.

1922 The Union of Soviet
Socialist Republics is
founded.

1924 Lenin's death on
24 January followed by
a power struggle (from
which Stalin emerges
victorious). St Petersburg
– which was renamed
Petrograd in 1914 –
becomes Leningrad.

1928 The first Five Year Plan
collectivises farms,
leading to famine and
the death of an estimated
five million.

1934 The assassination of
Sergey Kirov, Leningrad's
Party chief, heralds a

period of purges and
show trials.

1941 The Soviet Union enters
World War II. Leningrad is
under siege and German
troops reach the outskirts
of Moscow. Something
approaching 20 million
die during the war.

1953 Death of Stalin.

1956 Khrushchev's 'Secret
Speech' to the 20th Party
Congress denounces
Stalin and initiates a
limited and brief thaw.

1964 Khrushchev is replaced as
General Secretary of the
Soviet Communist Party
by Leonid Brezhnev.

1979 The USSR invades
Afghanistan.

1980 The Moscow Olympics
are boycotted by the USA.

1985 Mikhail Gorbachev
becomes Communist
Party General Secretary
in March and introduces
the policies of glasnost
(openness) and perestroika
(restructuring).

1986 Andrei Sakharov, human
rights campaigner, is
released from internal
exile.

1987   Boris Yeltsin is sacked as Moscow Party boss after openly attacking Gorbachev.

1989   First democratic elections take place. Revolutions throughout the Soviet bloc lead to the fall of the Berlin Wall.

1991   The citizens of Leningrad vote to restore the city's name to St Petersburg. After a failed communist coup, Yeltsin declares the Communist Party illegal. USSR dissolved, and Commonwealth of Independent States (CIS) formed in December. Gorbachev resigns on Christmas Day.

1992   'Shock therapy' introduced, abolishing price controls overnight on 2 January. Reform is deadlocked by parliament.

1993   In September the Russian parliament rebels after Boris Yeltsin suspends the constitution. Yeltsin loyalists eventually recapture the parliament building (White House). A new constitution is adopted in December.

1994   Yeltsin orders troops into the breakaway republic of Chechnya, suffering heavy losses militarily and in the opinion polls.

1996   In May protocol on Chechnya is signed. In July Yeltsin is re-elected. In December, last military units leave Chechnya.

1997   Yeltsin orders government to pay salaries and pensions. This is not met and unions threaten strikes. In May peace treaty is signed between Russia and Chechnya. Treaty signed between Russia and NATO. World Bank provides further loans.

1998   March crisis on Russia's stock markets. Rouble devalues rapidly and government is in crisis.

1999   In August, Chechen fighters make incursions into Dagestan. President Yeltsin names new Prime Minister – V V Putin. Some see this as a tactic to avoid prosecution after he leaves office. Russian forces return to Chechnya in answer to bomb attacks in Moscow. President Yeltsin finally gives up office.

2000 Vladimir Putin is elected president of Russian Federation. Disaster strikes Kursk nuclear submarine in Barents Sea. Britain and other NATO states offer to aid fast retrieval and save any survivors, but Russia refuses. Putin is criticised for this, but remains most popular politician in Russia.

2001 Russia supports US action in Afghanistan in retaliation for terrorist attacks on 11 September. This helps Russia justify anti-terrorist action in Chechnya.

2002 In October Chechen terrorists take more than 800 people hostage in the Dubrovka Theatre, Moscow. The subsequent assault by Special Forces goes wrong and 130 hostages die from the effects of gas.

2003 Celebrations marking the 300th anniversary of St Petersburg are attended by international politicians. Chechen suicide bombers kill 13 at a suburban rock festival in Moscow.

2004 In March President Putin is returned to power, winning more than 70 per cent of the popular vote. In August two Chechen suicide bombers evade security at Moscow's Domodedovo airport and blow up two passenger airliners, killing everyone on board. A week later a bomb kills ten in a Moscow metro station, and the following day Chechen terrorists enter a school in Beslan, North Ossetia, taking everyone hostage. Hundreds die in the ensuing rescue bid.

2005 In March, Chechen leader Aslan Mashkadov is killed by Russian special forces. In May more than 50 state and government heads attend the celebrations marking the 60th anniversary of the end of World War II. The same month the powerful former head of Yukos Oil, Mikhail Khodorovskiy, is found guilty of fraud and tax evasion and sentenced to nine years in prison. In August British air and sea rescue teams join the international effort to free seven crew members of a Russian mini-submarine trapped off the Kamchatka Peninsula.

Glorified in countless films, novels and paintings, the 'Great October Revolution' was more akin to a vaudeville farce than the dawn of the regime that was to grip Russia for over 70 years.

Vladimir Ulyanov 'Lenin' (1870–1924), in hiding and disguised by a badly fitting wig and glasses, desperately harangued his colleagues to start a revolution which most of them, including Stalin, were against. Despite their name, meaning 'The Majority', Lenin's Bolsheviks were few and only one of many opposition factions. Knowing that they had no

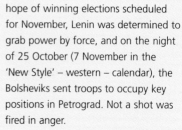

hope of winning elections scheduled for November, Lenin was determined to grab power by force, and on the night of 25 October (7 November in the 'New Style' – western – calendar), the Bolsheviks sent troops to occupy key positions in Petrograd. Not a shot was fired in anger.

Lenin penned a notice declaring the government deposed which was pasted around the city the next morning. Petrograd was unmoved: according to eyewitness accounts, offices and shops opened on time and opera-lovers looked forward to Chaliapin's evening performance at the Mariinskiy Theatre.

A haphazard siege of the Winter Palace, where the government unconcernedly sat on, was organised. Lenin emerged from hiding to make a short appearance at the Petrograd Soviet, the assembly of opposition parties, informing it that the worldwide socialist revolution had begun that night.

The 'storm' began at 9.40pm when a shot from the cruiser *Aurora*, moored downstream, broke the peace. But since the ship had just completed a refit, there were no live rounds and the revolutionaries had to make do with a blank shell.

Far from the frontal assault of grizzled workers, popularised in

Sergei Eisenstein's film *Days of October*, the first Bolshevik forces slipped into the building through open windows. The final death toll – five – resulted from stray bullets rather than spirited resistance by the Provisional Government, which was finally arrested and led away a little after 2am the following morning.

Left: Lenin mural on the Moscow metro
Above: Revolution Arch, VDNKh, Moscow
(*see p177*)

Politics

Steeped in ethnic conflict and economic chaos, the mighty Soviet Union lurched to an undignified halt on Christmas Day 1991, when Mikhail Gorbachev resigned the presidency of an extinct superpower. Over half a century of communist rule was over.

A subject for artists,
V V Putin

The *Ancien Régime*

Article 6 of the Soviet Union enshrined the role of the Communist Party and its 20 million members as 'the leading and guiding force of Soviet society'. Every farm and factory had its Party cell which supervised decisions emanating from the ruling Central Committee and Politburo. The nerve centre of the system, the Politburo met every Thursday under the guidance of the Party General Secretary, the country's leader.

The Party appointed all key officials, and its élite were rewarded with special medical care, access to closed shops and imported goods, country houses and hunting reserves. They were, in the subtle Russian distinction, *lyudi* rather than *naseleniye* – 'people' rather than 'population'. Their children could look forward to easy entry into the Party, university and the choicest jobs. The system, it seemed, was self-perpetuating.

The Beginning of the End

Lionised abroad for tolerating the destruction of the Berlin Wall in 1989, Gorbachev's popularity at home fell as his reforms ran into the sand. *Glasnost* assumed a momentum of its own, breaking the Party's monopoly of political power, sparking industrial unrest and unleashing pent-up ethnic tensions.

Instead of using it to resuscitate communism as Gorbachev had hoped, the people took *glasnost* at face value and pressed for ever wider freedoms. At the 1990 May Day parade in Red Square, Gorbachev was booed from the podium on Lenin's mausoleum.

Gorbachev met his nemesis in the democratically elected president of the Russian Republic, Boris Yeltsin, who used his mandate to declare Russian independence in June 1991, forcing Gorbachev to agree to the drafting of a new Union Treaty.

SOVIET LEADERS 1917–PRESENT

1917–22 Vladimir Ulyanov – 'Lenin'
1922–53 Joseph Djugashvili – 'Stalin'
1953–64 Nikita Khrushchev
1964–82 Leonid Brezhnev
1982–4 Yuri Andropov
1984–5 Konstantin Chernenko
1985–91 Mikhail Gorbachev
1991–9 Boris Yeltsin
2000– Vladimir Putin

The lower house of the Russian Parliament (Duma)

Transition to Democracy

Six months later, communism was gone and Russia was in turmoil. It had lost much of its 'empire' and, to make matters worse, fell into a war in Chechnya, which brought world criticism. The economy was stagnating and inflation skyrocketed, but those quick enough started to make their fortune by carving up the riches that were left. The West realised it needed stability in Russia, so immense loans were granted, to no avail.

Yeltsin's health deteriorated, governments came and went, and crisis deepened. It took a decade for Russia to pull itself out of chaos. War broke out again in Chechnya in 2000, but soon a popular president (no ordinary thing in Russia) came to power.

The Putin Era

A career KGB officer from St Petersburg who entered politics in the 1990s, Vladimir Putin called for a strong, united Russia, unashamed of its past. Economic liberalisation was to continue but with ultimate control increasingly in the hands of the state rather than private individuals. State power was also strengthened outside the capitals with the appointment of governors to rule 'super regions' in the President's name. The ruthless prosecution of the war in Chechnya signalled that independence movements would not be tolerated. The President's tough stance was undoubtedly popular in the country, as his resounding election victories in 2003 and 2004 showed. But liberals worry about the regime's authoritarian leanings, its control over the media and its inability to reduce the ever-widening gulf between rich and poor.

Detail from the Duma with the flag of the Russian Federation

Culture

Russians are fiercely proud of their deep cultural heritage, both in the arts and in daily life. Here peasant *joie de vivre* meets abstract philosophy, in a culture that has been moulded by centuries of foreign invasion, despotic government and Orthodox piety. There is no better introduction to it than a stay in Moscow or St Petersburg.

The famous Bolshoy Theatre, Moscow

The Arts

A love of the arts is by no means an élite diversion in Russia, where concerts and exhibitions are heavily subsidised and the national poet, Alexander Pushkin (1799–1837), is cherished with a passion far exceeding that of the English for Shakespeare or the Germans for Goethe.

Many artists enjoy a kind of cult status generally reserved in the West for pop stars. The reason is simple: under autocratic rule, producing subversive work carried the risk of imprisonment or exile if the tsar was displeased. Likewise, after 1917, artists denied membership of the official state union were liable to imprisonment as 'social parasites'. Their work would be secretly shared with trusted friends late in the evening around the kitchen table.

Russkaya Dusha

The 'Russian soul' – *russkaya dusha* – is more legend than fact, some say. At a time when burgers and BMWs are more in demand than balalaikas, the fabled Russian character can seem no deeper than the lacquer on the cheap nesting dolls sold at tourist flea markets.

But as many foreigners will agree, there is a certain quality to chance acquaintances in Moscow and St Petersburg that remains uniquely Russian. The quality is one of contradiction – a cross between public

Chess is very popular in Russia and no setting will prevent a quick game or two!

conformity and private dreams of anarchy, ruthless realism combined with sugary sentimentalism, striking rudeness on the street contrasted with overwhelming generosity to guests. Russians complain about the price of cabbages and wax lyrical about frost on the hawthorn in the same breath.

The Mir

One explanation is that most city-dwellers are only two or three generations removed from the countryside and its collectivist traditions. Outsiders are treated with suspicion, insiders are doted on and nonconformists are shunned: the Russian word for 'peasant community' is the same as that for the 'world' – *mir*.

Sometimes the result is plain bigotry. A streak of anti-Semitism runs deep in the national psyche, and even today a vocal element in every political demonstration blames everything from the October Revolution to the price of Coca-Cola on 'Zionist conspirators'.

Belief and Superstition

Despite decades of state-sponsored atheism, Russians are, in the widest sense, a strikingly religious people.

The Orthodox church is in full flourish again, as the shining new belltowers above the cities' rooftops testify. On a different level, from the adoration of Lenin to the post-Soviet fascination with television hypnotists and cure-all medicines, Russians have an unquenchable thirst for the improbable.

Westernisers and Slavophiles

Neither truly a part of Europe nor of Asia, Russia's fate has for centuries been hotly disputed between those who want to modernise the country on Western lines and those who believe in a distinct, Slavic, way forward. The two camps have agreed on only one thing – that an answer must be found to the eternal question: '*shto dyelat?*' ('What is to be done?'). Those *zapadniki* ('westernisers'), such as Peter the Great, who tried to turn Russia towards Europe, often did so with Asian barbarity. Meanwhile, the *slavyanofili* ('Slavophiles') declared Orthodox Russia's messianic role in the world but had no practical plan of action beyond extolling the peasant as a model of social organisation.

The debate is passionately pursued today as democrats battle for World Bank loans and European Union membership while nationalists and communists cry for a yet-to-be-defined Russian way.

Street art performances are frequent in Russia and provide an insight into all spheres of art

Haves and Have Nots

The Soviet Union was never the land of equality of socialist propaganda, despite the promises of Nikita Khrushchev that communism would be perfected by 1980. But when the system finally disintegrated, people were plunged into a confusing free-for-all. Now a few cruise the streets in Lincolns and Mercedes while the majority struggle desperately to make ends meet.

The poor get poorer …

… while the rich get richer

When artificially controlled prices were freed in 1992, inflation spiralled out of control. A pound sterling bought 140 roubles then; three years later, it bought almost 7,000. A two-tier society emerged and a bankrupt state could do nothing to help the losers: the monthly pension in late 1994 could be as little as 30,000 roubles, or about £6.

Underground stations were thronged with people selling bread, vodka, lottery tickets and ball-point pens late into the night. Qualified scientists, teachers and doctors resorted to selling souvenirs at tourist markets or importing cheap Chinese clothing to sell at home.

But the winners became very rich, very quickly. Whether communist-era

It is difficult not to feel sorry for the homeless children, but helping one will attract dozens of others

bureaucrats who retained their posts or mafia-like racketeers, they exploited the chaos of the market, making huge sums exporting oil and raw materials or taking a hefty percentage of business and restaurant turnovers. Russia's new breed of *biznismyen* lost little time in carving up the 'Wild East'.

As elsewhere, the rich get richer and the poor get poorer. In big cities, though, the middle class is increasing. Shops are not just for the rich any more, but frequented by 'ordinary' people, many of whom are becoming quite content. Those who work in foreign or private companies earn decent money in Russian terms, and can afford foreign holidays, one or two cars and a decent living standard.

To be rich in Russia means to be incredibly rich – according to one recent estimate, 25% of the national wealth is in the hands of just 100 individuals, and there are more billionaires in Moscow

than anywhere in the world. And while it is true that under President Putin the political power of the tycoons has declined, they still wield enormous economic clout. Remote from ordinary life, they live their lives within the confines of their luxurious villas and dachas, venturing out only to broker deals or to party with celebrities in exclusive nightclubs.

To be poor in Russia means to be incredibly poor. Many live on the streets due to alcoholism, drug abuse, eviction or unemployment. Unqualified workers have no chance of another job. Pensions are so low that, if old people have no family to take care of them, they have to resort to begging. It is not uncommon to see old men and women wearing medals for heroism while begging on the street corner from people for whose freedom they once fought.

Where did all the good intentions of the Gorbachev era go awry? The likely answer is *Bog znaet* – 'God knows'.

Entertainment for top-class citizens is available on almost every street corner

First Steps

It takes a little courage to choose Russia for a holiday.
Though the country has more or less learnt how to deal
with modern tourism, it still has its strange alphabet, strict
bureaucrats and ever-present police checking the
documents of passers-by. Yet a thoroughly rewarding trip
is well within the grasp of any visitor armed with a sense of
humour and a few ground rules.

Russian architecture at its
best

The Price of Change

Take personal security seriously. Today's
Russia is an exhilarating, brutal and
frequently bewildering place and it pays
to have your wits about you. Wear a
money belt under your clothing and keep
cameras and other valuables close to your
person. Watch out for pickpockets,
especially on the metro and in other
crowded places. Give money-changers
and other hustlers a wide berth, and –
one final precaution – make photocopies
of your passport and visa and note down
credit card details, including emergency
phone numbers, in case of loss.

Even in winter Russia has its magic

Moscow and St Petersburg can no
longer be regarded as cheap destinations;
indeed, Moscow was recently voted the
fourth most expensive city in the world.
The free market has created a society
with a burgeoning middle class, but one
in which the disparity in wealth between
the very rich and the very poor is vast.
For visitors this means expensive hotel
bills and restaurant prices on a par with
those of London, Paris or New York.
Foreigners are also expected to pay well
above the local going rate for admission
to museums, theatres and other
attractions. There are still bargains to be
had, however, while some things, notably
public transport, remain downright
cheap.

The jury is also out on Putin's
handling of the economy. While
inflation remains low, foreign debt
continues to fall and growth rates are
impressive (largely due to high world
energy prices), the gap between rich and
poor is grotesque. Almost one third of
Russians live below the poverty line,
unemployment is rising, the health
service is disintegrating, life expectancy
is falling and the birth rate is in decline.

When to Visit

There can be nothing more Russian than the crisp frosts of winter, ice on the Neva and snow falling upon the golden cupolas of Moscow's churches. Likewise, there can be nothing more unpleasant than permanently frozen fingers and wet feet. To avoid too much of the latter, the best time for a winter trip is late November through to early January before the really heavy frosts or the slush of the March thaw.

In the warmer season, July and August can be suffocating in both Moscow and St Petersburg. The air is fresher around May and September, and, if the weather holds, these are perhaps the most attractive times of the year. To catch the legendary St Petersburg White Nights, when the sun virtually never sets and the whole city celebrates, plan your trip for the end of June or beginning of July.

Renovations are under way to improve your enjoyment of many interesting sites

Moscow's busy Leningrad railway station, the terminus for trains to St Petersburg

Visas and Arrival

All foreign nationals require a visa to
enter Russia which will only be issued
on a full passport. Bear in mind when
planning your trip that the process of
issuing a visa can be extremely lengthy
and subject to unpredictable delays.
Make sure you leave yourself sufficient
time before departure to cover all
eventualities – as much as a month.

Arrival at the airport can go
smoothly, but it is best to prepare for
lengthy queues at passport control and
customs. There is a green channel at the
customs barrier, but hard currency is
declarable; if you bring more than
£1,800 (about $3,000), you must queue
at the red channel anyway. You must fill
in an immigration card: the official
keeps one half and you keep the other
with you. On it goes your temporary
registration stamp, compulsory for stays
exceeding 72 hours. Customs and
temporary-stay rules change often, so
check carefully beforehand.

Members of tour groups or guests of
Western-style hotels will probably be
met at the airport. Everyone else must
negotiate a taxi ride to their destination
with the dozens of private cab drivers
waiting in the arrivals hall. (*See
Arriving, p178, for more information.*)

Coping with the Language

Nothing will increase the pleasure and
ease of your trip to Russia more than a
few hours at home spent mastering the
Cyrillic alphabet. Although the task
seems daunting, the value later is
immeasurable for working out metro
stations and street names (few signs
are bilingual in St Petersburg; none

Moscow Metro

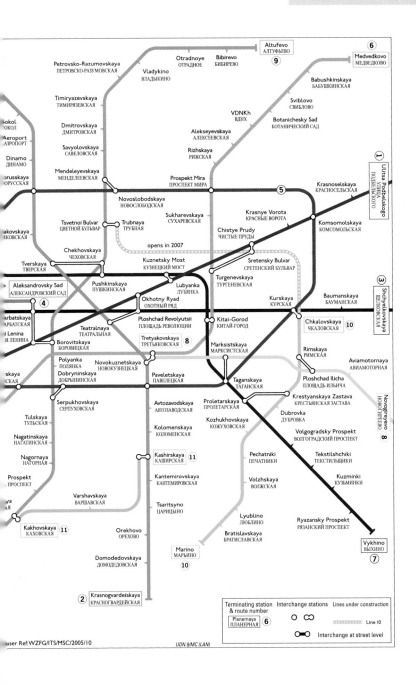

Petrovsko-Razumovskaya
ПЕТРОВСКО-РАЗУМОВСКАЯ

Otradnoye
ОТРАДНОЕ

Bibirevo
БИБИРЕВО

Altufevo
АЛТУФЬЕВО

9

6

Medvedkovo
МЕДВЕДКОВО

Vladykino
ВЛАДЫКИНО

Babushkinskaya
БАБУШКИНСКАЯ

Timiryazevskaya
ТИМИРЯЗЕВСКАЯ

Sviblovo
СВИБЛОВО

Sokol
ОКОЛ

Aeroport
АЭРОПОРТ

Dmitrovskaya
ДМИТРОВСКАЯ

VDNKh
ВДНХ

Botanichesky Sad
БОТАНИЧЕСКИЙ САД

Dinamo
ДИНАМО

Savyolovskaya
САВЁЛОВСКАЯ

Alekseyevskaya
АЛЕКСЕЕВСКАЯ

orusskaya
ОРУССКАЯ

Rizhskaya
РИЖСКАЯ

Mendeleyevskaya
МЕНДЕЛЕЕВСКАЯ

Prospekt Mira
ПРОСПЕКТ МИРА

5

Krasnoselskaya
КРАСНОСЕЛЬСКАЯ

1

Ulitsa Podbelskogo
УЛИЦА ПОДБЕЛЬСКОГО

Novoslobodskaya
НОВОСЛОБОДСКАЯ

Sukharevskaya
СУХАРЕВСКАЯ

Krasnye Vorota
КРАСНЫЕ ВОРОТА

Komsomolskaya
КОМСОМОЛЬСКАЯ

akovskaya
КОВСКАЯ

Tsvetnoi Bulvar
ЦВЕТНОЙ БУЛЬВАР

Trubnaya
ТРУБНАЯ

Chistye Prudy
ЧИСТЫЕ ПРУДЫ

opens in 2007

Chekhovskaya
ЧЕХОВСКАЯ

Kuznetsky Most
КУЗНЕЦКИЙ МОСТ

Sretensky Bulvar
СРЕТЕНСКИЙ БУЛЬВАР

Tverskaya
ТВЕРСКАЯ

Turgenevskaya
ТУРГЕНЕВСКАЯ

Baumanskaya
БАУМАНСКАЯ

3

Shchyolkovskaya
ЩЁЛКОВСКАЯ

Aleksandrovsky Sad
АЛЕКСАНДРОВСКИЙ САД

4

Pushkinskaya
ПУШКИНСКАЯ

Lubyanka
ЛУБЯНКА

Okhotny Ryad
ОХОТНЫЙ РЯД

Kurskaya
КУРСКАЯ

rbatskaya
АРБАТСКАЯ

i Lenina
И ЛЕНИНА

Teatralnaya
ТЕАТРАЛЬНАЯ

Ploshchad Revolyutsii
ПЛОЩАДЬ РЕВОЛЮЦИИ

Kitai-Gorod
КИТАЙ-ГОРОД

Chkalovskaya
ЧКАЛОВСКАЯ

10

Borovitskaya
БОРОВИЦКАЯ

Tretyakovskaya
ТРЕТЬЯКОВСКАЯ

8

Marksistskaya
МАРКСИСТСКАЯ

Rimskaya
РИМСКАЯ

Aviamotornaya
АВИАМОТОРНАЯ

Polyanka
ПОЛЯНКА

Novokuznetskaya
НОВОКУЗНЕЦКАЯ

Paveletskaya
ПАВЕЛЕЦКАЯ

Taganskaya
ТАГАНСКАЯ

Ploshchad Ilicha
ПЛОЩАДЬ ИЛЬИЧА

skaya
СКАЯ

Dobryninskaya
ДОБРЫНИНСКАЯ

Novogireyevo
НОВОГИРЕЕВО

8

Serpukhovskaya
СЕРПУХОВСКАЯ

Avtozavodskaya
АВТОЗАВОДСКАЯ

Proletarskaya
ПРОЛЕТАРСКАЯ

Krestyanskaya Zastava
КРЕСТЬЯНСКАЯ ЗАСТАВА

Tulskaya
ТУЛЬСКАЯ

Kolomenskaya
КОЛОМЕНСКАЯ

Kozhukhovskaya
КОЖУХОВСКАЯ

Dubrovka
ДУБРОВКА

Nagatinskaya
НАГАТИНСКАЯ

Volgogradsky Prospekt
ВОЛГОГРАДСКИЙ ПРОСПЕКТ

Nagornaya
НАГОРНАЯ

Kashirskaya
КАШИРСКАЯ

11

Pechatniki
ПЕЧАТНИКИ

Tekstilshchiki
ТЕКСТИЛЬЩИКИ

Prospekt
ПРОСПЕКТ

Kantemirovskaya
КАНТЕМИРОВСКАЯ

Volzhskaya
ВОЛЖСКАЯ

Kuzminki
КУЗЬМИНКИ

ya
Я

Varshavskaya
ВАРШАВСКАЯ

Tsaritsyno
ЦАРИЦЫНО

Kakhovskaya
КАХОВСКАЯ

11

Orekhovo
ОРЕХОВО

Lyublino
ЛЮБЛИНО

Ryazansky Prospekt
РЯЗАНСКИЙ ПРОСПЕКТ

Bratislavskaya
БРАТИСЛАВСКАЯ

Vykhino
ВЫХИНО

Marino
МАРЬИНО

10

7

Domodedovskaya
ДОМОДЕДОВСКАЯ

2

Krasnogvardeiskaya
КРАСНОГВАРДЕЙСКАЯ

Terminating station
& route number

Interchange stations

Lines under construction

Planernaya
ПЛАНЕРНАЯ

6

Line 10

Interchange at street level

Moscow's transport is very efficient, but first you need to get 'the hang of it'

is in Moscow). You will also be able to pronounce words and destinations – Russian is basically a phonetic language and most words are spoken just as they are spelled.

A handful of polite words learnt at home will go a long way towards melting the icy glare of even the most unhelpful official.

(*See pp184–5 for an introduction to basic words and phrases.*)

Organising your Time

Moscow and St Petersburg offer an astounding range of sights and activities for even the most demanding visitor. You will only be able to cover a fraction of them in the course of a normal trip, so it is worth sorting out priorities in advance. Most of the major sights in both cities are conveniently grouped near the centre; some, such as the Kremlin or the Hermitage, require most of a day to do them justice. Minor points of interest, such as less well-known museums and

churches, are often spread far apart and the travelling involved is easy to underestimate. Don't feel obliged to trudge from one landmark to another – remember to save some enthusiasm for that trip to the ballet, five-course meal or ice-hockey game in the evening!

Orientation

Moscow is planned like a cartwheel with major arteries branching out from the Kremlin (*Kreml*) and linked by a series of concentric ring roads. The first is the Bulvar (Boulevard Ring), which starts and stops at (but does not cross) the Moscow river, on either side of the Kremlin. The next ring road is the Sadovaya (Garden Ring), a heaving multilane highway encircling the city centre. (Note: it does *not* coincide with the circle line of the metro.) Recently a *Tretya Koltsovaya* (Third Ring) was added.

Finally, the Outer Ring Road (MKAD – Moskovskoye Koltsevaya Avtodoroga) defines the city's limits far on the outskirts of town.

St Petersburg is simpler, with most points of interest grouped on, around or at the ends of Nevskiy Prospekt, the city's backbone.

Driving

Driving around Moscow and St Petersburg is technically possible but not recommended.

Little has changed since the 19th century when the writer Nikolai Gogol observed 'What Russian does not love fast driving? How could his soul, which is so eager to whirl round and round, to forget everything in a mad carousel, to exclaim sometimes: To hell with it all! … How could his soul not love it?'

Russians overtake on both sides, aim for gaps in the traffic which do not exist and mercilessly refuse to give way to timid foreign drivers. In addition, the roads are riddled with potholes and governed by an extremely arcane highway code.

For the undaunted, there are plenty of car rental agencies in both cities.

(*See p180 for more information.*)

The Unpredictable

Economic and political turmoil has only added to the ever-present element of unpredictability in Russian life. Prepare

Typical blue street sign, Moscow's Tver Street

to find museums unexpectedly closed for renovation. Do not be surprised if a favourite restaurant slides dramatically down- or upmarket in the course of a week; nor if the exchange rate does the same. Anticipate that booking offices may be closed, as the sign will say, 'for technical reasons'. Be prepared to be denied access to an apparently public bar for not knowing the right people. It is all part of the adventure.

Yeliseev's, Moscow's historic gourmet food store on Tverskaya Ulitsa: luxury if you can afford it

It is better to use the metro to avoid daily traffic jams and confrontation with traffic police

Public Transport

As in any city, getting the hang of the public transport system in Moscow and St Petersburg takes practice. While you can conceivably do without using it, a few tactical stops on the metro (underground) network will dramatically save time and energy between sights. Buses, trams and trolleybuses are trickier to master, but where essential, they are mentioned in the text. To begin with, try trolleybuses Nos 10 and 13 for negotiating Moscow's Garden Ring, while in St Petersburg, Nos 1 and 7 cut out the footwork on Nevskiy Prospekt. (*See pp186–7 for detailed information on travelling by public transport.*)

Many sights are located close to metro stations (above shows Moscow's Pushkin Museum of Fine Arts close to Kropotkinskaya metro station)

St Petersburg Metro

A Communicarta
Style 45 design

Komendantskiy Prospekt
КОМЕНДАНТСКИЙ ПРОСПЕКТ

Staraya Derevnya
СТАРАЯ ДЕРЕВНЯ

Krestovskiy Ostrov
КРЕСТОВСКИЙ ОСТРОВ

Chyor

Chkalovskaya
ЧКАЛОВСКАЯ

Petrog

Gorkovska

Sportivnaya
Спортивная

ПРИМОРСКАЯ
3 Primorskaya

ВАСИЛЕОСТРОВСКАЯ
Vasileostrovskaya

Sadovaya САДОВАЯ

Baltiiskaya БАЛТИЙСКАЯ

ТЕХНОЛ

Narvskaya НАРВСКАЯ

Tekhno

КИРОВСКИЙ ЗАВОД
Kirovsky Zavod

Avtovo АВТОВО

ЛЕНИНСКИЙ ПРОСПЕКТ
Leninsky Prospekt

ПРОСПЕКТ ВЕТЕРАНОВ
Prospekt Veteranov | 1

○ ○—○   Interchange with other lines

ДЕВЯТКИНО
Devyatkino | 1   Terminating station & route number

© Communicarta Ltd

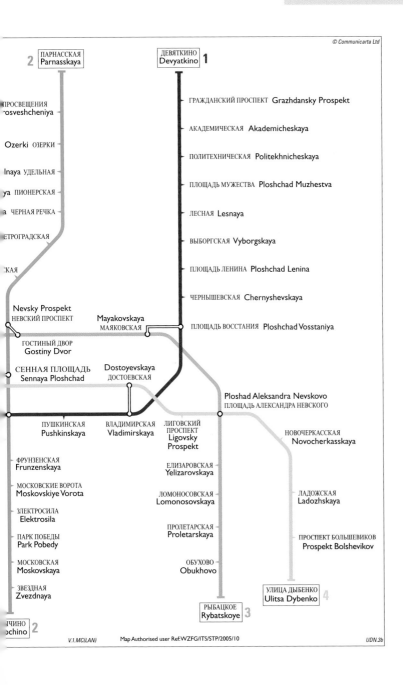

2 ПАРНАССКАЯ Parnasskaya

1 ДЕВЯТКИНО Devyatkino

ПРОСВЕЩЕНИЯ osveshcheniya

Ozerki ОЗЕРКИ

Inaya УДЕЛЬНАЯ

уа ПИОНЕРСКАЯ

а ЧЕРНАЯ РЕЧКА

ЕТРОГРАДСКАЯ

КАЯ

ГРАЖДАНСКИЙ ПРОСПЕКТ Grazhdansky Prospekt

АКАДЕМИЧЕСКАЯ Akademicheskaya

ПОЛИТЕХНИЧЕСКАЯ Politekhnicheskaya

ПЛОЩАДЬ МУЖЕСТВА Ploshchad Muzhestva

ЛЕСНАЯ Lesnaya

ВЫБОРГСКАЯ Vyborgskaya

ПЛОЩАДЬ ЛЕНИНА Ploshchad Lenina

ЧЕРНЫШЕВСКАЯ Chernyshevskaya

Nevsky Prospekt НЕВСКИЙ ПРОСПЕКТ

Mayakovskaya МАЯКОВСКАЯ

ПЛОЩАДЬ ВОССТАНИЯ Ploshchad Vosstaniya

ГОСТИНЫЙ ДВОР Gostiny Dvor

СЕННАЯ ПЛОЩАДЬ Sennaya Ploshchad

Dostoyevskaya ДОСТОЕВСКАЯ

Ploshad Aleksandra Nevskovo ПЛОЩАДЬ АЛЕКСАНДРА НЕВСКОГО

ПУШКИНСКАЯ Pushkinskaya

ВЛАДИМИРСКАЯ Vladimirskaya

ЛИГОВСКИЙ ПРОСПЕКТ Ligovsky Prospekt

НОВОЧЕРКАССКАЯ Novocherkasskaya

ФРУНЗЕНСКАЯ Frunzenskaya

ЕЛИЗАРОВСКАЯ Yelizarovskaya

МОСКОВСКИЕ ВОРОТА Moskovskiye Vorota

ЛОМОНОСОВСКАЯ Lomonosovskaya

ЛАДОЖСКАЯ Ladozhskaya

ЗЛЕКТРОСИЛА Elektrosila

ПРОЛЕТАРСКАЯ Proletarskaya

ПАРК ПОБЕДЫ Park Pobedy

ПРОСПЕКТ БОЛЬШЕВИКОВ Prospekt Bolshevikov

МОСКОВСКАЯ Moskovskaya

ОБУХОВО Obukhovo

ЗВЕЗДНАЯ Zvezdnaya

УЛИЦА ДЫБЕНКО Ulitsa Dybenko **4**

ЧИНО ochino **2**

РЫБАЦКОЕ Rybatskoye **3**

M o s k v a (M o s c o w)

'Moscow! How much is combined in this sound for the Russian heart!' wrote the national poet Alexander Pushkin in the 19th century. The city is the capital and one of the cultural focuses of Russia, enshrining civic ceremony and the Orthodox faith, great musical traditions and theatrical excellence. Most of all, it is the incarnation of that subtle blend of anarchy and nostalgia which the nation proudly refers to as the 'Russian Soul'.

Detail of a typical Russian church tower

A Fight for Survival

Since its humble inception in 1147 as a small encampment overlooking the Moskva River, Moscow has suffered frequent attack. First came the Mongols – or Tartars – who sacked the city, gathered slaves and collected tribute from the residents. Fear of the 'Tartar yoke' lasted until the 16th century – they last levelled the city in 1571. Next came the Poles, who occupied the city for two years at the beginning of the following century.

Relative peace ensued as St Petersburg assumed the mantle of imperial capital until, in 1812, Napoleon entered the Kremlin. A desperate population resorted to setting the city ablaze to drive him out. Finally, in 1941, Hitler boasted: 'In a few weeks, we shall be in Moscow. I will raze that damned city and in its place construct an artificial lake with central lighting.' He failed.

The Old and the New

As capital of the Soviet Union, Moscow grew rapidly from a picturesque, medieval city into a sprawling, modern metropolis. Soviet planners blasted away old quarters of the city to erect massive hotels and force through multilane highways. Stalin ordered the construction of the vast Gothic skyscrapers which today dominate the skyline.

But Moscow retains plenty of its old character and remains a Russian, rather than Soviet, city. Whole streets are lined with the

The Historical Museum on the famous Red Square

neo-Classical mansions of the old aristocracy. Wandering into a back alley off the main roads can be like entering a time warp as you stumble across delicate Orthodox churches and courtyards little changed from the time of Tolstoy and Dostoevsky.

The Muscovites

Russia is a land of over 100 separate nationalities, from Tuvans to Kalmyks and Chukchi to Circassians, as well as the Russians themselves. A true Muscovite is a rare individual indeed. But whatever their origin, the ten million or so inhabitants of Moscow are proud of their city, for all its eccentricities and hardships.

Some say that Muscovites unjustly perceive themselves as the nation's top crop. Whether this is true or not, visitors must judge for themselves. As Muscovites like to say, there are Russians and there are Muscovites.

Moscow Town Plan

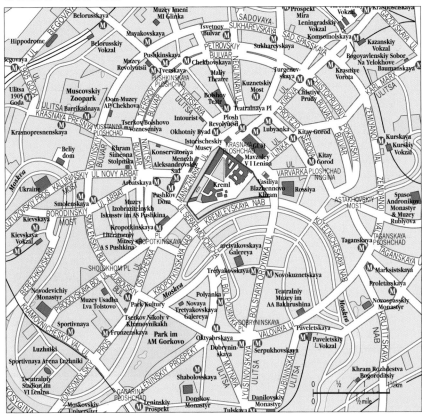

ALEKSANDROVSKIY SAD (ALEXANDER GARDENS)

Tucked under the Kremlin's western wall, the Alexander Gardens are best known for the solemn Tomb of the Unknown Soldier. The gardens were laid out for Tsar Alexander I in 1821 over the bricked-in Neglinnaya river – which might account for the characteristic coolness they afford in summer after a hot afternoon's visit to the Kremlin. *Manezhnaya Ulitsa. Free. Metro: Aleksandrovskiy Sad, Biblioteka imeni Lenina.*

The Tomb of the Unknown Soldier with its eternal fire

Borovitskaya Ploshchad (Borovitskaya Square)

Adjoining the southern end of the gardens, this busy intersection is dominated by the striking Pashkov Dom (Pashkov House), built between 1784 and 1786. It now shares some of the 29 million volumes of the neighbouring Biblioteka imeni Lenina (Lenin Library), Europe's largest library.

Manezhnaya Ploshchad (Manège Square)

The low, columned building alongside the upper half of the gardens is the former imperial riding school, or Manège. Destroyed by fire in March 2004, it has since been rebuilt and is open for exhibitions. (*See also p85.*)

Memorial Mogila Neizvestnovo Soldata (The Tomb of the Unknown Soldier)

The memory of World War II is deeply felt in Russia. Estimated at 20 million, the number of Soviet deaths will never be precisely known. Official delegations and newlyweds lay wreaths here on the grave of an infantry man killed at the 41km ($25^1/_2$ miles) point on Leningradskoye Shosse (Leningrad Highway), the closest German soldiers came to Moscow. The inscription beneath the eternal flame reads: 'Your name is unknown, your deeds immortal.'

Old Russian architecture paid a lot of attention to details

Obelisk

Under Lenin's orders, the first of countless memorials to the Revolution was unveiled in the Alexander Gardens in 1918. It was previously a monument celebrating the tercentenary of the Romanov dynasty, but the Bolsheviks knocked off the double-headed eagle and inscribed the names of socialist thinkers.

BELIY DOM (WHITE HOUSE)

Gleaming on the banks of the river opposite the Stalinist skyscraper Ukraine Hotel, the White House stands at the heart of the battle for Russia's political future. As the House of Soviets of the Russian Federation, it was the site of makeshift barricades against the abortive 1991 coup, when crowds swamped half-hearted tank commanders sent in to restore order.

In October 1993, this time as the Russian Parliament, the building was the focus of hostilities between President Yeltsin and hardline deputies. It looked, briefly, as though the communists were triumphant until Yeltsin ordered tanks to bombard the building into submission: 138 people were killed. Repairs cost over $80 million (£48 million).

Graffiti, pockmarked walls and crucifixes to the fallen mark the battle zone today on the backstreets behind what is now a heavily fenced-off House of the Russian Government.
Konyushkovskaya Ulitsa. Metro: Krasnopresnenskaya.

HOTEL MOSCOW

The decision of City Mayor, Yuri Luzhkov, to allow the demolition of the Hotel Moscow in 2003 continues to be the subject of fierce controversy. Constructed in 1933–5 at the height of the Stalin era, the hotel was considered by many to be the Art-Deco masterpiece of Soviet architect, Aleksey Shchusev. The site was purchased by the US Decorum Corporation, which is building a new hotel on similar lines to the old.

DIEHARD COMMUNISTS

The statue of Karl Marx opposite the Bolshoy Theatre and the former Lenin Museum on Ploshchad Revolyutsii are favourite gathering points of diehard communists (*metro: Ploshchad Revolyutsii*). Mostly pensioners, the true believers are now more of a tourist sight than a real political force. Demonstrations take place most Sundays, but the really big crowds gather on 7 November (Revolution Day) and May Day.

The White House, home to the Russian Parliament

Churches and Cathedrals

Travellers in the 19th century never ceased to be amazed at the sight of Moscow's myriad golden cupolas – said by tradition to number '40 times 40' – and the incomparable sound from her belfries as the call to prayer rang across the city. Hundreds of churches were demolished or ransacked under the Soviets; today the Orthodox religion is in the throes of a powerful surge in popularity and most of the capital's finest holy buildings are already restored to their pre-Revolutionary splendour.

Detail of a cathedral and the Orthodox Crucifix

The most interesting churches and cathedrals not covered elsewhere in the text are listed below.

Bogoyavlenskiy Sobor na Yelokhove (Yelokhovskiy Cathedral)
By legend the birthplace of the holy fool St Basil, the cathedral (originally built in the 13th century, completed in 1845) is among Moscow's most revered, serving as the patriarch's headquarters after his ejection by the communists from the Kremlin in 1918. The atmosphere of the resplendent interior during an evening service is unforgettable.
Ulitsa Yelokhovskaya (Spartakovskaya) 15. Tel: 267 7591. Metro: Baumanskaya.

Khram Pokrova na Filyakh (Church of the Intercession at Fili)
Although for long not a working church, this is well worth a visit as one of the most striking examples of Muscovite High-Baroque architecture. Icons from the Rublyov Museum of Ancient Russian Culture and Art are on permanent display within.

Novozavodskaya Ulitsa, 10 minutes' walk north from Metro Fili. Open Wed–Mon 11am–5pm. Closed 1st Fri of month. Admission charge.

Khram Rozhdestva Bogoroditsiy (Church of the Nativity of the Virgin)
This tiny church was once part of the neighbouring Simonov monastery

The elegant façade of Yelokhovskiy Cathedral

A WORD ON ETIQUETTE

While Russians are tolerant of curious foreigners entering their churches, they do expect a few simple rules to be observed. Modest dress is expected (shorts and T-shirts are frowned upon) and women should wear a headscarf while men should remove hats. You can take photographs when there is no religious service, but only after obtaining a permit from the official on duty. Noise should be kept to a minimum. You may enter and leave during services – most last several hours and are held standing. Hence the not-so-devout are looked upon with indulgence.

erected by Russia's patron saint, Sergiy Radonezhskiy. When the monastery was part levelled to make way for the vast Zil works, the church was somehow left in the middle of the factory grounds. It is one of Moscow's most ancient churches, dating from 1509.
Ulitsa Vostochnaya 6. Tel: 275 7011.
Metro: Avtozavodskaya.

Khram Simeona Stolnika (Church of St Simon Stylites)
It is the juxtaposition of this little church against the monolithic tower blocks of the Novy Arbat that makes the building – bare inside after years of service as the All-Russia Nature Conservancy Society exhibition hall – a photographic favourite. Built in 1649, the church had its moment of glory with the wedding in 1801 of the fabulously rich Count Sheremetev to one of his serfs.

Ulitsa Vorovskovo 5. Tel: 291 2184.
Metro: Arbatskaya.

Tserkov Bolshovo Vozneseniya (Church of the Grand Ascension)
This monumental church (1840) witnessed the wedding of Alexander Pushkin and was beloved of Tchaikovsky for its marvellous acoustics. The Soviets vandalised it thoroughly, converting it by turn into a workshop, garage and lightning conductor research laboratory.
Ulitsa Bolshaya Nikitskaya 36.
Metro: Arbatskaya.

Tserkov Nikoly v Khamovnikakh (Church of St Nicholas of the Weavers)
One of Moscow's best-loved – and gaudiest – churches, St Nicholas dates from the 17th century, when it was commissioned by the city's weavers. As eye-catching as the exterior is the decoration inside – preserved because the church remained open during Soviet rule.
Ulitsa Lva Tolstovo 2. Tel: 246 6952.
Metro: Park Kultury.

Exterior decoration on the colourful Church of St Nicholas of the Weavers

CATHEDRAL OF CHRIST THE SAVIOUR

Being next to the Kremlin and the largest cathedral in Moscow, this huge church is hard to overlook. It was originally built to commemorate the defeat of Napoleon in 1812 and work began in 1839. There were a number of sites which were considered for this cathedral, but the emperor Nicholas I chose the hill above the Moscow river. Before construction works could commence Alekseyevskiy Convent and the Church of all Saints had to be removed from the site. Consecrated on 26 May 1883, the coronation day of Alexander III, it was 103m (338ft) high and its rich interior covered 6,805sq m (73,250sq ft) and could hold 10,000 people. The main dome was 25.5m (84ft) across.

It survived the Revolution, but its central position on a hill overlooking the river was too good to ignore. In 1931 it was torn down on Stalin's orders for one of his megalomaniac projects, a Palace of the Soviets. This palace was meant to be the highest building in the world and was to become a monument to Lenin and the victory of socialism. Massive propaganda preceded the destruction of the cathedral where the communist regime marked it as 'totally inartistic' and 'misplaced'. In the end the palace was never started and a swimming pool was built instead, but this was plagued by problems and later closed.

After the fall of communism, the mayor of Moscow led the project to erect a replica of Khram Khrista Spasitelya, using modern materials and methods. It has become Moscow's main cathedral, visited by leading public figures including President Putin. The cornerstone for the new cathedral was laid in 1990 and construction work and work on the frescos lasted through to 1999, when the cathedral was consecrated once again.

The cathedral interior holds three altars. The main altar is dedicated to the Birth of Our Lord and the two side altars to Saint Nicholas and Alexander Nevskiy. One main distinction between the 'new' and the 'old' cathedral is that the 'new' cathedral is placed on a crypt which replaced the initial hill it stood on. Inside the crypt are the Church of Holy Transfiguration, the Hall of Church Councils, the Hall of the Holy Synod, several dining halls, a patriarchal suite and offices and garages for church staff.

Entry is free, but visitors are expected to behave appropriately (*see p35*). The park around the cathedral has many benches where you can rest your legs while watching ships on the Moskva River. *Open daily 6.30am–10pm.*
Tel: 203 3823. Admission free.

The majestic Cathedral of Christ the Saviour dominating and overlooking the Moscow River

Galleries and Exhibitions

Moscow has a wealth of galleries including some, such as the Pushkin Fine Arts Museum, of world-wide reputation. But the city is also at the centre of a boom in contemporary art, as new freedoms of artistic expression have brought an explosion of avant-garde talent.

Moscow is a city of art

See English-language press for current listings.

A-3 Galereya (A-3 Gallery)

One of Moscow's best, this gallery is at the leading edge of the city's modern art scene.
Starokonyushenny Pereulok 39. Tel: 291 8484. Open: 11am–7pm. Closed: Mon, Tue. Admission free. Metro: Smolenskaya.

Galereya Guelman (Guelman Gallery)

One of the leading lights of Moscow's contemporary art world, Marat Guelman exhibits the cream of the capital's artists. See the informative website for the latest details on exhibitions and sales.
Malaya Polyanka 7/7. Tel: 238 8492. www.guelman.ru. Open: Tue–Fri noon–7pm, Sat noon–6pm. Admission free. Metro: Polyanka.

Galereya Shishkin (Shishkin Gallery)

Leonid Shishkin has been collecting since the *glasnost* era, 1989 to be precise. His specialities are Russian art works of the 19th and early 20th century and post-war Soviet painting.
Neglinnaya 29. Tel: 200 1951. www.shishkin-gallery.ru. Open: Mon–Sat 11am–8pm. Admission free. Metro: Tsvetnoy Bulvar.

MARS Galereya (MARS Gallery)

This gallery in a western suburb has built a reputation as one of Moscow's foremost exhibition centres of contemporary works. The founders were among those whose exhibitions were famously bulldozed by the authorities in the 1970s. Not all works here are of the highest quality, but all are interesting and inspiring. Work is regularly on sale and credit cards are accepted.
Malaya Filyovskaya Ulitsa 32. Tel: 146 2029. Open: noon–8pm. Closed: Mon. Admission free. Metro: Pionerskaya.

Musey Izobrazitelnykh Iskusstv imeni A S Pushkina (Pushkin Fine Arts Museum)

While the Pushkin Museum has good collections of classical and Egyptian antiquities and copies of Renaissance sculpture, it is best known for its rich holdings of European painting – especially the French Impressionists – second only to the Hermitage in St Petersburg (*see pp102–5*). The upper floor contains important works by Cézanne, Manet, Monet, Gauguin, Matisse and Picasso (rooms 17–18 and 21). Earlier European artists, including Rembrandt, Rubens, El Greco and Botticelli, are well represented.

The museum rocked the art world in 1995 when it showed for the first time paintings plundered from private collections by Soviet troops at the end of World War II, including *Carnival* by Goya, Manet's *Portrait of Rosita Maury*, El Greco's *St Bernard* and *Portrait of Madame Choquet at the Window* by Renoir. Many had been written off as lost masterpieces. Whether the paintings will remain in the museum is a matter of diplomatic debate: the Ambassador of Germany, from where most of the works were taken, first knew of their existence when he received an invitation to the exhibition's opening day, and the embassy has since demanded their return.
Ulitsa Volkhonka 12. Tel: 203 9578. www.museum.ru/gmii. Open: 10am–7pm. Closed: Mon. Admission charge. Tours in English are available. Metro: Kropotkinskaya.

Novaya Tretyakovskaya Galereya (New Tretyakov Gallery)

The back half of the Central Artist's House (*see below*) hosts temporary exhibitions from the collections of the Tretyakov Gallery proper. Its main exhibition centres on Russian art of the 20th century.
Tel: 238 1378. Open: 10am–7pm. Closed: Mon.

Phototsentr (Photo Centre)

One of Moscow's most consistently interesting photographic galleries shows regular exhibitions of Russian and some foreign photojournalism.
Gogolevskiy Bulvar 8. Tel: 290 5685/6996. Open: noon–8pm. Closed: Mon. Admission charge. Metro: Kropotkinskaya.

Tretyakovskaya Galereya (Tretyakov Gallery)

See pp64–5.

Tsentralniy Dom Khudozhnika (Central Artists' House)

This huge building opposite the gates of Gorky Park is Russia's premier exhibition centre of contemporary art from all over the country. The gallery grounds are now the resting place of many of Moscow's revolutionary statues: a kind of communist elephants' graveyard.
Krymskiy Val Ulitsa 10. Tel: 238 9634. www.cha.ru. Open: daily except Mon, 11am–8pm. Admission charge. Metro: Park Kultury.

The Central Artists' House, home of contemporary Russian art

Krasnaya Ploshchad (Red Square)

Witness to holy processions, executions, grandiose military parades and bloody insurrections, the vast, cobbled expanse of Red Square is the spiritual heart of both capital and nation. At the far end, the visitor's eye is drawn by the fantastic cupolas of St Basil's Cathedral, quintessential symbol of Moscow.

Detail from the Tomb of the Unknown Soldier

A bustling market place in early times, the square saw Ivan the Terrible beg forgiveness for his misdeeds and Peter the Great personally undertake the beheading of his foes. 'Krasnaya' in old Russian meant 'beautiful', and it is only recently that the square became identified with 'red' communism.
Metro: Ploshchad Revolyutsii/Okhotniy Ryad.

Gum

Privatised, and officially known as the 'Upper Trading Rows', this glorious shopping arcade opposite the Kremlin is still affectionately known by its Soviet acronym, standing for 'State Department Store'. Completed in 1888, its bridges and balconies afford a bird's-eye view of the shopping frenzy below.

Kazanskiy Sobor (The Kazan Cathedral)

Constructed in 1636 in honour of the miraculous 'Mother of God of Kazan' icon that helped rid Muscovy of the Poles, Kazan Cathedral was destroyed by Stalin 300 years later to erect public toilets. Detailed plans kept in secret were used to rebuild it. The patriarch blessed it in 1993.
Open: daily 8am–7pm.

Lobnoe Mesto

While the origins of the name are unclear, the history of Muscovy's ancient tribune is dramatic. In 1613, the first of the Romanov dynasty, Mikhail, was here proclaimed tsar; the leader of the 1682 peasants' revolt, Stenka Razin, was led along the street now bearing his name to be quartered on the site; and Peter the Great reputedly executed the first ten of the 2,000 rebellious palace guard here in 1698.

Mavzoley V I Lenina (Lenin's Mausoleum)

See p49.

Minin-Pozharskiy

The statue outside St Basil's depicts the Nizhny Novgorod butcher Minin persuading Prince Pozharskiy to lead the army of liberation on Moscow and drive out the occupying Poles. It was commissioned in a flush of nationalism after 1812 and completed in 1818. Reliefs show the collection of funds and final surrender of the Poles in 1612.

St Basil's Cathedral at the lower end of Red Square is probably the most photographed site in Moscow

Nulevoiy Kilometr (Zero Kilometre)
In front of the rebuilt Resurrection Gate to Red Square is the 'zero kilometre' plaque. From here all Russian roads are measured. Visitors drop coins on it to ensure safe travel in Russia.

Spasskaya (The Saviour's Tower)
Broadcast on the radio at daybreak, midday and midnight, the bells of the Saviour's Tower, erected in 1491, defined the Soviet worker's day. Under Stalin, the *Internationale* chimed out over Red Square. The small tower alongside was built for Ivan the Terrible so that he could watch executions in comfort.

Vasiliya Blazhennovo Khram (St Basil's Cathedral)
Napoleon referred to the cathedral as 'that Mosque' and stabled his horses here during the invasion of 1812. Whatever one's taste, there is no denying the motley splendour of the Cathedral of the Intercession of the Virgin, better known as St Basil's after the 'holy fool' famed for his denunciation of Ivan the Terrible and buried in one of the chapels.

Ivan decreed work on the building to begin following the capture of the Khanate of Kazan: legend has it that he had the architects' eyes put out on completion in 1555 to prevent them creating anything more beautiful.

The central chapel reaches a height of 57m (187ft) and the surrounding eight are built to strict geometric design. The exterior was originally white and gold, the present vivid colour scheme being added in the 17th century. The interior is more understated, but it is well worth wandering the convoluted corridors to see the recently restored frescos and icons.

Open: 11am–6pm (11am–4pm, winter). Closed: Tue and first Mon of each month. Admission charge.

Kreml (The Kremlin)

All highways in Russia lead to the gates of this, the very hub of imperial and, latterly, Soviet might. To the visitor it is an unnerving place, where the sublime beauty of a medieval cathedral coexists with the terror of a historic torture tower.

Detail from one of the Kremlin's cathedrals

The Kremlin dates back to 1156, shortly after Moscow was founded. In 1367, Prince Dmitri Donskoy pulled down the wooden bailey and erected limestone battlements. These in turn were replaced at the end of the 15th century by vast walls, up to 19m (62ft) high and 6.5m (21ft) in width. They were commissioned by Tsar Ivan III ('The Great') and, like some of the cathedrals, are the work of Italian architects who were assisted in their labours by Russian craftsmen.

CATHEDRALS
The heart of the Kremlin is the flag-stoned expanse of Sobornaya Ploshchad (Cathedral Square), the spiritual focus of Imperial Russia. Site of royal weddings, coronations and christenings, it is the final resting place of many of the tsars. Admission to the cathedrals is included in the general ticket to the Kremlin.

Arkhangelskiy Sobor (Cathedral of the Archangel Michael)
Dedicated to the patron of the Princes of Muscovy, the cathedral was built in 1508. A team of over 100 artists from all over the kingdom was enlisted to paint the frescos of ancient Russian warriors. Several early tsars are entombed here, including Mikhail, first of the Romanovs, and Ivan the Terrible (the latter out of sight behind the iconostasis, since he was excommunicated by the patriarch).

Blagoveshchenskiy Sobor (Cathedral of the Annunciation)
Built in 1489, the tsars' private church, paved with jasper and capped with nine cupolas, contains 16th-century biblical frescos and one of Russia's most precious iconostases. From the chapel to the right Ivan the Terrible, forbidden by Orthodox law to enter the church itself, watched proceedings through a partition.

Cathedral of the Assumption, the largest on the Cathedral Square

Patriarshiy Palaty and Sobor Dvenadtsati Apostolov (Patriarch's Palace and Cathedral of the Twelve Apostles)

The palace is now a Museum of 17th Century Life and Applied Art with a superb display of period furniture, gold and silver ware and ornate church vestments rescued from Kremlin monasteries destroyed by Stalin. At the end of the exhibition is the tiny Cathedral of the Twelve Apostles.

Tserkov Rizpolozheniya (Cathedral of the Deposition of the Robe)

A private chapel, this church (1655) is decorated with 17th-century frescos and holds a small woodcarving museum.

Uspenskiy Sobor (Cathedral of the Assumption or Dormition)

The cathedral (1479) houses the tombs of all the patriarchs up to 1700. Look for the Throne of Monomakh made for Ivan the Terrible. In 1989 it held the first religious service in the Kremlin since 1918.

Kreml Plan

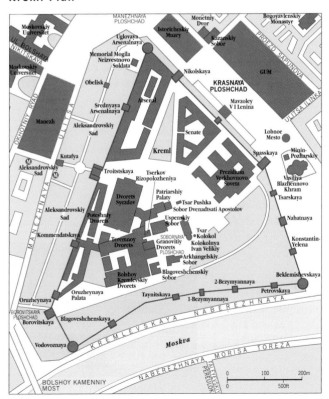

OTHER SIGHTS
Kolokolnya Ivan Velikiy (Ivan the Great Bell Tower)

For long the tallest structure in Moscow, the 81m (266ft)-high Ivan the Great Bell Tower (1600) dominates Cathedral Square. The tower commands a 40km (25 mile) view across the capital yet its foundations are little more than 4m (13ft) deep. It was initially part of Tserkov Ioana Lestvichnika (Church of St John Climacus). Today 18 of the original 36 bells remain.

Oruzheynaya Palata (The Armoury)

One of the high points of a Kremlin tour is the fabulous wealth on show in the Armoury building. There is a stunning exhibition of treasures such as the battle helmet of Mikhail, first of the Romanov dynasty, and the ivory throne of Ivan the Terrible. Seize the chance to see the collection of jewelled Easter eggs created by Carl Fabergé for the tsar's family. An additional fee gains entrance to the State Diamond Fund, a collection of some of the world's most fantastic gemstones. *The Armoury is closest to the Borovitskaya Gates entrance. Admission by separate ticket. Tours 10am, noon, 2.30pm, 4.30pm.*

Towers

Of the Kremlin's 20 towers, the Konstantin-Yelena Tower was a torture chamber and the Blagoveshchenskaya (Annunciation) Tower was used as a prison. The small Tsarskaya (Tsar's) Tower beside the Spasskaya Gates used to be a wooden pavilion from which Ivan the Terrible watched executions on Red Square. The rotating red stars atop each of the towers, made from Ural Mountains' rubies, were erected in 1937 in place of the tsarist two-headed eagle.

Tsar Kolokol and Tsar Pushka (Tsar Bell and Cannon)

The Tsar Bell – at 210 tonnes the world's largest – was cast in 1735 but proved too heavy to hoist and was never rung. Similarly, the Tsar Cannon, intended to defend the Kremlin's Spasskaya Gates, was never fired. Cast in 1586, it boasts an 890mm calibre.

Open: 10am–5pm except Thur. Tel: 203 3776 or 203 0349. www.kremlin.museum.ru. Admission charge. Enter through the Kutafya Tower in the Alexander Gardens (tour groups through the Borovitskiy Gate). Note that the entire Kremlin closes with little warning for state occasions. Guidebooks and audio guides are available from the ticket office. For private guided tours *tel: 203 0349.* If you hire a local guide (many of them stand around the entrance to the Kremlin) they may help obtain 'sold-out' tickets to the Armoury and Diamond Fund. *Metro: Aleksandrovskiy Sad.*

The world's largest cannon – Tsar Pushka

The Armoury

Bolshoy Kremlevskiy Dvorets (Great Kremlin Palace)

Overlooking the river, the tsars' Moscow residence was built for Nicholas I in 1849. The royal apartments have been preserved in pre-Revolutionary splendour. Communist leaders lay in state in the Giorgiesvskiy Zal (St George's Hall). Restricted access.

Dvorets Syezdov (State Kremlin Palace)

The key speeches of Gorbachev's *perestroika* were delivered in the 6,000-seat auditorium of this fiercely modern building (1961) also used as a second venue for the Bolshoy opera and ballet.

Granovitaya Dvorets (Palace of Facets)

The squat Palace of Facets (1491) once formed part of the Grand Duke of Muscovy's stone residence. It was later used as a banqueting hall and for the celebrated transvestite balls held by the wildly extravagant Empress Elizabeth (reigned 1741–61). Restricted access.

Prezidium Verkhovnovo Soveta, Senate and Arsenal (Praesidium of the Supreme Soviet, the Senate and the Arsenal)

To the left as you look from the Palace of Congresses is the state Arsenal, built in the early 18th century to Peter the Great's plan. Over 800 captured French cannon ring the building's pediment.

In the centre stands the former Senate building (1787), once headquarters of the Soviet government and now housing the presidential administration. To the right is the former Praesidium of the Supreme Soviet.

Teremnoy Dvorets (Terem Palace)

Built originally for Tsar Mikhail Romanov, this is perhaps the Kremlin's most spectacular building. The interior seems to owe more to fairytale Baghdad than 17th-century Moscow with its low vaulted ceilings, lavish gilding, ornate tilework and stained-glass windows. Restricted access.

Street Life

Russian cities are a source of contrast, but life on the streets is not as shady as it was. Gone are the days when every hotel entrance was crowded by beggars, illegal money changers, pickpockets and crooks. The homeless and street urchins are hardly seen; if they do appear they tend not to bother strangers. Old women begging near churches are tolerated and even pitied.

Since the fall of communism, things have improved for most people in the cities: wages have gone up a little and people seem more content. They have also got used to foreign visitors: today, central Moscow is full of tourists, diplomats and students. City streets no longer display the chaos and poverty of the communist years.

Now they are a place where life can be enjoyed to the full. In summer, streets are dotted with beer- or coffee-gardens, many providing live music until late at night. People relax by taking long walks through the city centre, and resting on park benches or next to fountains. Street entertainment is alive and well, with musicians playing anything from Tchaikovsky to modern rock.

Street traders offering 'genuine' war medals, icons, souvenirs and bootleg CDs are an endangered species, though. They have all been forced to move to official markets, partly by new city regulations and partly because Russians have taken to the Western concept of huge, air-conditioned shopping centres.

People also breathe more easily on Moscow's boulevards, which now differ little from those of Western cities. It is an unforgettable and romantic experience to sit in a restaurant's garden near the historic walls of the Kremlin and listen to a band playing your favourite songs. The atmosphere – combined with the mellowness of a late Moscow evening and good food and drink – is amazing.

Moscow's roads may have improved, but its traffic has rules of its own and they are quite puzzling for those who do not know them. The main rule is that there are no rules. However, pedestrian tunnels are frequent and they offer perfect acoustics for street musicians and outdoor studios for portrait painters. Street life seems to have come out of its cocoon.

The transformation to a cosmopolitan capital is complete. Services for foreigners are offered at almost every street corner. The city centre is safe even in the evening and there are many police officers on the streets. All the same, Moscow is a metropolis and has a high crime rate, so adequate caution is advised.

Above left: The riverbank provides a good setting for long walks
Bottom left: Muscovites head for a park every opportunity they get
Above: Fishing is another favourite pastime
Below: There are many opportunities to shop for 'original' souvenirs

Red Moscow

Changes in the political climate have seen the axing of funds allocated to maintaining the Lenin industry; where once you could not take two steps without being reminded of the 1917 Revolution's mastermind, Lenin is slowly slipping off Moscow's map. Street names have largely reverted to their ancient originals and the huge Central Lenin Museum on Ploshchad Revolyutsii, which boasted over 50 million visitors, has been returned to the city authorities. Still, there remain a few spots that shed light on one of history's greatest, if infamous, figures.

Moscow's metro portrait of Gorky

Lubyanka (The Lubyanka)

Lenin established the KGB's forerunner – the CheKa – in the Rossiya Insurance building on Lubyanskaya Ploshchad. *Pravda* outlined his policy of terror in 1918: 'Do not demand incriminating evidence to prove that the prisoner has opposed the Soviet government ... Your first duty is to ask him to which class he belongs ... This question should decide the fate of the prisoner.'

Successor organisations to the CheKa, like the NKVD, became the instrument of Stalin's crackdown on real and imaginary Party opposition in the 1930s. Many of the victims disappeared through the back gates of the dour Lubyanka building on Furkasovskiy Pereulok: torture and execution took place in the courtyard and basement. Between five and seven million were arrested in the Great Purge of 1937–8 alone, most ending up – and dying – in the Gulag Archipelago of prison camps.

The poem *Requiem* by Anna Akhmatova (1888–1966) vividly recalls the systematic repression of the purges. 'I have learned how faces fell to bone, how under the eyelids terror lurks,

Lubyanka – headquarters of the regime and a symbol of 'red terror'

The Mausoleum – tomb of a man who changed the life of millions

How suffering inscribes on cheeks the hard lines of its cuneiform texts ...'
The Lubyanka remained a symbol of repression until 1991 when it was the scene of demonstrations, culminating in the toppling of the statue of CheKa founder, Felix Dzerzhinskiy – and symbolically the Soviet regime.
Lubyanskaya Ploshchad. Metro: Lubyanka.

Mavzoley V I Lenina (Lenin's Mausoleum)

A week after his death, Lenin's wife Krupskaya wrote to *Pravda* imploring: 'Do not build memorials to him or palaces to his name. Do not organise pompous ceremonies in his memory.' Her pleas went unanswered and the result is the granite and porphyry ziggurat, designed by the distinguished Soviet architect, Aleksey Shchusev.

Bedecked in a polka-dot bow tie, Lenin is maintained in his crystal sarcophagus by a computer-controlled ventilation system and a yearly bathing with a chemical cocktail. The honour guard at the gates was abolished by Yeltsin, but changing political fortunes have put on hold plans to clear the site. Thousands of old communists still gather here on 22 April to celebrate their idol's birthday.

The Kremlin wall behind the building is the ex-USSR's principal necropolis. Here, with Stalin and other Bolshevik luminaries, lie Yuri Gagarin, the first man in space, and the American chronicler of the Revolution, John Reed.
Krasnaya Ploshchad. Tel: 923 5527.
Open: Wed, Thur, Sat, Sun 10am–1pm. Admission free.
Metro: Ploshchad Revolyutsii, Okhotniy Ryad.
Bags and cameras must be checked in at the Historical Museum.

Komsomolskaya station

THE METRO

Moscow's metro system is reputedly
the world's most efficient but rates as a
'must' among the capital's tourist sights
for the less prosaic reason that many
stations are architecturally as stunning
as anything on offer above ground.
*Open: daily 6am–1am. See pp24–5 for
Metro map and p186 for public transport
details.*

Underground Palace

At 7am on 15 May 1935, Mr Lakyshev
of the Red Proletariat factory bought a
ticket at Sokolniki station and became
the first of over 77 billion passengers to
ride Moscow's celebrated metro.

The metro was planned by Stalin as a
showpiece of communist engineering,
capable of transporting the city's
workers rapidly and in the lap of

SOME STATISTICS

Every day, 506 escalators (137,814 steps)
at 150 stations carry over 8 million
passengers to 7,840 trains that travel 244km
(151 miles) of track and consume 4 million
kWh of electricity.

---

socialist luxury. The older stations are
the most impressive, heavily decorated
with marble, stucco and crystal.

A Pick of the Stations

Kievskaya: designed to celebrate the
friendship of the Russian and Ukrainian
peoples, the mosaics were completed at
a time when forced collectivisation by
Stalin killed millions in the Ukraine.
Komsomolskaya: honouring Soviet
youth, this palace of gold, marble and
florid stucco depicts scenes from
Russian history.
Mayakovskaya: completed in 1938 to a
prize-winning design by Aleksey
Dushkin, the station is named after the
poet and playwright, Vladimir
Mayakovskiy (1893–1930). Features to
look out for include the mosaics on the
theme of aviation and sport.
Park Kultury: originally the terminus of
the Sokolniki line, the bas-reliefs depict
workers at leisure, playing chess, skating,
reading and dancing.
Ploshchad Revolyutsii: this station
celebrates the Great October Revolution
of 1917 with 36 heroic bronze figures,
paired under each of its 40 arches. They
depict the major contributors to the

Lenin, yesterday's hero

founding of the Soviet state, from sailors and young pioneers to architects and sportsmen.

Wartime Metro
Constructed to double as air-raid shelters, many of the stations are extremely deep underground. In 1941 Stalin addressed deputies in Mayakovskaya on the anniversary of the Revolution and had an office at Chistiye Prudy in the Air Defence Command outpost – reached by a secret door behind the bust of Kirov.

Besides the metro, Moscow is riddled with other tunnels. Some link with the former KGB's headquarters, while those beneath the White House and the Kremlin are reportedly wide enough to drive a car down.

Traurny Poezd Lenina (Lenin's Funeral Train)
The train which transported Lenin's body from his country estate Gorki (*see p83*), after his death on 21 January 1924, is displayed in a large pavilion beside the Paveletskiy railway station. An inscription outside claims that, though Lenin is dead, his memory will live forever, as will his ideas and actions. If the pavilion is closed, the train can still be seen through the glass windows.
Paveletskiy Ploshchad 1. Open: 10am– 6pm Mon to Fri; 10am–4pm Sat. Free. Metro: Paveletskaya.

VLADIMIR ILYICH ULYANOV – 'LENIN' (1870–1924)

Born in the southern city of Simbirsk (now Ulyanovsk), Lenin took up radical politics in earnest after his brother was executed for attempting to assassinate the tsar. Much of his life was spent exiled in Europe, quarrelling in cafés with the many other émigré socialists. He looked 'more like a provincial grocer than a leader of men' according to one British agent, but what marked Lenin out from the rest was his genius for seizing the moment. Smuggled into Russia by the Germans during World War 1, he and his tiny 'Bolshevik' ('majority') party grabbed power in more of a farcical coup than a revolution. As his partner Leon Trotsky remarked, 'Power was lying in the streets.' Lenin simply picked it up.

Monasteries and Convents

Before the Revolution, Russia's 5,000 or more monasteries and convents were the focal points of traditional life. Many of the most splendid were in Moscow. Of those that survived the communist onslaught, some remain in ruins or converted into factories and workshops, but many are now slowly returning to life, their newly-gilded churches recalling past glories.

Novodevichiy Monastyr on the banks of the Moscow River

Danilovskiy Monastyr (Danilov Monastery)

Moscow's most ancient monastery dates from 1282 and is named after its founder, Prince Daniel, son of Alexander Nevsky. After use as a juvenile delinquents' prison, it resumed its role as the headquarters of the Orthodox Patriarchate in 1988 (hence its spruce appearance). The oldest church within is the 17th-century Church of the Holy Fathers, containing Daniel's relics, and packed with worshippers on church festivals. Beggars throng the Church of Simeon Stylites at the monastery entrance – giving to the poor is a central element of the Orthodox faith, which is observed punctiliously today.

Entrance is free but, as in all Russian religious buildings, modest dress and respectful behaviour is expected.
Danilovskiy Val 22. Tel: 955 6787. Open: daily 8am–8pm. Metro: Tulskaya.

Donskoy Monastyr (Don Monastery)

Patriarch Tikhon was kept under arrest by the Bolsheviks in the monastery's Old Cathedral where his tomb now lies. The Don Monastery is also the resting place of many of Moscow's aristocrats,
including the wealthy Golitsyn family who are buried in the Church of the Archangel Michael in the monastery grounds.

The oldest buildings and fortress walls date from the 16th century when the monastery was founded by Boris Godunov in honour of the Don Mother of God icon, whose miraculous powers were believed to have helped defeat the Crimean Tartars. The original icon is now in the Tretyakov Gallery (*see pp64–5*). Today the monastery is once again operative.
Donskaya Ploshchad 1. Tel: 232 0221. Open: daily 7am–dusk. Metro: Shabolovskaya.

Novodevichiy Monastyr (Convent of the New Maidens)

Peter the Great banished his sister Sophia to a cell in this breathtakingly beautiful ensemble, for alleged participation in a revolt. The Austrian ambassador watched in horror as the culprits were tortured and hung before her window: 'Nobody will easily believe how lamentable were their Cries and Howls, unless he has well weighed their Excruciations and the Greatness of their Tortures.'

The convent's most notable buildings are the red-brick bell tower (1690) and the central Smolensk Cathedral (1525) containing stunning frescos and Sophia's tomb. A number of exhibitions occupy the lesser buildings.

The adjoining cemetery is Moscow's most prestigious and the site of the graves of the writers Anton Chekhov and Nikolai Gogol, film director Sergei Eisenstein and – curiously – Communist Party General Secretary Nikita Khrushchev, removed from power in disgrace in 1964 and hence denied a plot in the Kremlin wall (*see p49*). You can buy a guide to the cemetery at the entrance gates.

In good weather, the view of the complex from across the lake is unforgettable.

Novodevichiy Proezd 1. Convent – tel: 246 8526; cemetery – tel: 246 6614. Open: daily except Tue, 10am–5pm. Admission charge. Metro: Sportivnaya.

Novospasskiy Monastyr (Novospasskiy Monastery)

This pretty monastery (1490) on a lakeside hill by the Moskva River, has a sinister past. It has been a children's prison, a sobering-up centre for arrested female drunks, and a base of the NKVD secret police, forerunner of the KGB. Summary executions were carried out in the monastery yards – mass graves of the victims were discovered in the banks beneath the monastery towers after the complex was surrendered to the church in 1991.

The central Cathedral of the Transfiguration (1647), built as the family church of the Romanov dynasty, now holds services again.

Krestyanskaya Ploshchad 10. Tel: 276 9570. Open: 8am–8pm. Metro: Proletarskaya.

Iconostasis in Donskoy Monastery church

Museums

Moscow has a well-developed museum culture. Museums display unique exhibits that are difficult to find elsewhere. Some museums lack English labelling on exhibits, but a tour, in English, may be requested in many of them. Moscow's streets are dotted with museums covering every imaginable topic. The following is only a small selection of what's on offer.

Dom Romanovikh

Borodinskaya Bitva Panorama (Borodino Battle Panorama)

Desperate Russian resistance scotched Napoleon's expectations of an easy victory on the fields of Borodino in 1812, a battle celebrated in this vast panorama. The huge losses suffered on both sides made Borodino a symbol of Russia's struggle against foreign invasion.
Kutuzovskiy Prospekt 38. Tel: 148 1967. Open: Sat, Sun noon–6pm; other times by arrangement. Admission charge. Metro: Kutuzovskaya.

Dom Romanovikh (Romanov House)

Built by the grandfather of Tsar Mikhail, the first of the Romanov dynasty, this elegant city residency has been restored as a museum of 16th- and 17th-century aristocratic life.
Ulitsa Varvarka 10. Tel: 298 3706. Open: Mon, Thur 10am–5pm; Wed 11am–6pm. Closed Tue and 1st Mon of the month. Admission charge. Metro: Ploshchad Revolyutsii.

Lubyanka 12 (Security Service Museum)

Located in the old KGB social club, this fascinating museum aims to polish the tarnished image of the Russian security services. The exhibits include CheKa leader Felix Dzerzhinskiy's desk, cameras and other spy paraphernalia, revolvers and contraband seized by the KGB's successor, the FSB.
Lubyanka 12. Open for guided tours only by Patriarshy Dom Tours, tel: 795 0927. Metro: Lubyanka.

Muzey Dekorativno-Prikladnovo Iskusstva (Applied Arts Museum)

A stunning exhibition of traditional arts including jewellery, ceramics and superb-quality lacquered boxes.
Ulitsa Delegatskaya 3. Tel: 923 7725. Open: 10am–6pm. Closed: Fri and the last Thur of the month. Admission charge; tickets sold until 5pm. Metro: Tsvetnoy Bulvar.

Muzey Drevnerusskoi Kultury i Iskusstva imeni Andreya Rublyova (Rublyov Museum of Ancient Russian Culture and Art)

You will find a rich display of religious art displayed in the Andronnikov Monastery and can also visit the museum's adjoining restoration studios.
Andronyevskaya Ploshchad 10. Tel: 278 1489. Guided visits tel: 248 1467.

The Polytechnic Museum offers a large exposition from various spheres of technology

Open: 11am–6pm. Closed: Wed and the last Fri of each month. Admission charge. Metro: Ploshchad Ilyicha.

Muzey Istorii Goroda Moskvy (Museum of the History of Moscow)

The systematic destruction of religion in the capital is but one of the themes illustrated by this collection of prints, lithographs and archaeological bits and pieces relating to Moscow's chequered history and occupying the former Church of St John the Evangelist.
Novaya Ploshchad 12. Tel: 924 8490/923 9830. Open: 10am–6pm, Fri and Wed 11am–7pm. Closed: Mon. Admission charge. Metro: Lubyanka.

Muzey Izobrazitelnykh Iskusstv imeni A S Pushkina (Pushkin Fine Arts Museum)

See pp38–9.

Muzey Kosmonavtov (Space Travel Museum)

Situated beneath the massive titanium rocket monument at VVTs, the museum contains a modest collection of space hardware ranging from early satellites to the spacesuits of the first cosmonaut, Yuri Gagarin, and a number of the dogs (now stuffed) blasted into orbit prior to Gagarin's flight.
Pervaya Ostankinskaya Ulitsa 41/9. Tel: 283 7914. Open: 10am–6pm. Closed: Mon and last Fri of month. Admission charge. Metro: VDNKh.

Muzey Revolyutsii (Museum of the Revolution)

Rather than close down what was once a centrepiece of tourist-orientated propaganda, the curators have produced an even-handed tour through the convulsions of Russia's revolutionary past. The exhibits range from bold communist posters to a tableau of the barricades of 1991 as the Soviet Union drew its final gasps for survival.
Tverskaya Ulitsa 21. Tel: 299 5217/ 299 6724. Open: Tue–Sat 10am–6pm, Sun 10am–5pm. Closed: Mon and last Fri of month. Admission charge. Metro: Tverskaya.

The Armed Forces Museum displays weapons that were once a menace to the West

Muzey Vooruzhonnykh Sil (Armed Forces Museum)

Full of the hardware with which Soviet leaders threatened to 'bury the West', this excellent museum also contains memorabilia of the Red Army's most famous victories. The remains of Gary Power's U2 spyplane, shot down in 1960, are also here. For more of the same, *see pp66–7*.
Ulitsa Sovetskoy Armii 2. Tel: 281 4877. Open: Wed–Sun 10am–4.30pm. Admission charge. Metro: Prospekt Mira.

Muzey Vostoka (Museum of the East)

In a building dating from 1821, this museum takes us for a trip to the East, each country distinguished by a different-coloured background. Archaeological discoveries from the Caucasus and Asia are displayed alongside presents from China, North Korea and Iran. Almost impossible to describe, the displays are as colourful and as diverse as the cultures themselves.
Muzey Vostoka, Nikitskiy Bulvar 12a. Tel: 291 9614/4966. Open: Tue–Sun 11am–7pm. Admission charge. Metro: Arbatskaya.

Politekhinicheskiy Muzey (Polytechnic Museum)

A little rusted and loose at the seams, the displays on the achievements of Soviet science and industry are still worth a visit on a rainy day. Some exhibits are labelled in English. There are many models of mining, nuclear and other machinery. It is a must for all interested in science, chemistry or technology.
Novaya Ploshchad 3/4. Tel: 923 0756. Open: 10am–6pm. Closed: Mon and the last Thur of the month. Metro: Lubyanka/Kitay Gorod.

HOUSE MUSEUMS

Moscow is littered with museums in homes of the great and the good. Clocks are stopped at the time of death and the rooms and effects preserved as found. With shifting financial priorities, many have been closed, but those dedicated to the following should survive:

Maxim Gorky

Despite his serious misgivings about the 1917 Revolution, Gorky (1868–1936) was lionised by the state as a pillar of proletarian literature and promoted as a model for young Soviet writers. Coaxed

back from emigration and disillusion in 1928, Gorky lived in a wonderful example of Russian avant-garde architecture till his death, rumoured to be at Stalin's prompting.
Muzey Kvartira im Gorkovo – Ulitsa Malaya Nikitskaya 6/2. Tel: 290 0535. Open: Wed, Fri noon–6.30pm; Thur, Sat and Sun 10am–4.30pm. Free admission. Metro: Arbatskaya/Pushinskaya.

Alexander Pushkin

The reverence reserved for Russia's premier poet (1799–1837) – almost as for a saint – far exceeds that of the English for Shakespeare and the Germans for Goethe. It is evidenced in the hushed awe with which local visitors pore over the author's collected manuscripts, jottings and possessions gathered in two museums, the second of which was Pushkin's home for a short time.
Literaturniy Muzey A S Pushkina, Ulitsa Prechistenka 12. Tel: 201 5674. Open: Wed, Fri–Sun 10am–6pm; Thur noon–
7pm. Closed: Mon, Tue and last Fri of the month. Metro: Kropotkinskaya. Dom Muzey A S Pushkina, Arbat 53. Tel: 241 9295. Open: Wed–Sun 11am–6pm. Closed: last Fri of the month. Metro: Smolenskaya.

Lev Tolstoy

The life, works and philosophy of the grand old man of Russian literature (1828–1910) are celebrated in two Moscow museums. Despite Tolstoy's espousal in later life of such doctrines as vegetarianism and pacifism, his stature was such that even the strict censors of communist aesthetics were forced to leave his works and memory untouched. The Muzey-Usadba Lva Tolstovo, a timbered house where Tolstoy lived between 1882 and 1901, is especially evocative and a must see.
Muzey L N Tolstovo, Ulitsa Prechistenka 11. Tel: 201 5811. Metro: Kropotkinskaya. Muzey-Usadba Lva Tolstovo, Ulitsa Lva Tolstovo 21. Tel: 246 9444. Open: Tue–Sun 10am–6pm. Metro: Park Kultury.

Viktor Vasnetsov

One of the leaders of the Wanderers' artistic movement at the turn of the last century, Vasnetsov (1848–1926) is still much loved for his nostalgic renditions of Russia's mythical past. The interiors are superb.
Dom-Muzey Khudozhnika V M Vasnetsova, Vasnetsova Pereulok 13. Tel: 281 1329. Open: Tue–Sun 10am–5pm. Closed: last Thur of the month. Metro: Sukharevskaya.

Gorky's Art-Nouveau house

The Artistic Explosion

In the late 19th and early 20th centuries, Russia was gripped by a momentous revolution in the arts which paralleled the turbulent atmosphere of the times. The spirit was one of experiment, a true *fin de siècle* rejection of outmoded doctrines and dusty prejudices.

In 1863, exasperated by its enforced adherence to classical subjects, 14 artists walked out of the St Petersburg Academy of Arts and formed their own group, known as 'The Wanderers' – *Peredvizhniki* – for their travelling exhibitions. Their work dealt innovatively with social issues, epitomised by the searching pictorial parables of Ilya Repin.

Artists were now being supported by Russia's growing class of businessmen, like the railway magnate Savva Mamontov (*see p88*) and the merchant Pavel Tretyakov, whose collection of

Russian art forms the heart of the Tretyakov Gallery (*see pp64–5*).

The 'World of Art' – *Mir Iskusstva* – movement at the turn of the 20th century was driven by the impresario Sergei Diaghilev, whose aim was to 'exalt Russian art in the eyes of the West'. Members such as Alexander Benois, Leon Bakst and Valentin Serov not only galvanised Russian Impressionism and Art Nouveau, but also designed sets and costumes for Diaghilev, whose Ballets Russes took Europe by storm. The inspired choreography of Michel Fokine and

breathtaking dancing of Anna Pavlova and Vaslav Nijinsky, combined with the extraordinary scores of Igor Stravinsky's *Firebird* and *Rite of Spring*, revolutionised ballet.

The Moscow Art Theatre sprang to prominence with the plays of Anton Chekhov and their interpretation by Konstantin Stanislavsky, whose concentration on naturalness gained world-wide renown as the Stanislavsky Method.

Throughout the years surrounding the 1917 Revolution, Russian artists, like Mikhaíl Larionov, Natalya Goncharova and Kazimir Malevich, were the undisputed leaders of the avant-garde.

Movements mushroomed: Primitivism, Rayonnism, Futurism, Supremacism, Constructivism ...

The poet of the Revolution, Vladimir Mayakovsky, declared: 'We do not need a dead mausoleum of art where dead works are worshipped, but a living factory of the human spirit.' His contemporaries followed his lead, committing themselves wholeheartedly to the great communist experiment which, by the 1930s, had silenced them all.

Left: Tretyakovskaya Gallery, known for its valuable exhibits
Above: The Bolshoi Theatre, famous for staging opera and ballet performances

The tip of the Ostankino TV tower

Ostankino

Painstaking restoration is slowly returning to its former glory the 18th-century summer estate of Count Nikolai Sheremetev, one of Russia's richest and most cultured noblemen. Not all the property is open to the public, but the nearby Ostankino TV tower and the Tekhnopark fully justify a trip out from the centre of town.

OSTANKINO SERF ESTATE
Italianskiy Pavilion (Italian Pavilion)
The theatre is flanked by two antechambers, the Italian and Egyptian Pavilions, the first of which is open to visitors. The hand-printed wallpaper, gilded woodwork and stucco ornamentation hint at the luxurious premises enjoyed by the count's privileged guests.

Ostankinskiy Krepostnoi Teatr (Ostankino Theatre)
During Ostankino's heyday, the road from Moscow was lit at night by braziers for those invited to the count's legendary soirées, the focus of which was his famous Serf Theatre.

The daughter of a serf blacksmith, Praskovya Kovalyova-Zhemchugova took to the stage at the age of 11. Breaking all the taboos of high society, Count Sheremetev fell in love with her and freed her from bondage. Catherine the Great forbade the relationship, but on her death Sheremetev prevailed on her son Paul I and the couple were married in 1801. Unfortunately Praskoya died two years later of tuberculosis: the Sklifosovskiy Hospital for the Poor in Moscow was founded in her memory.

The theatre hall is in the main body of the building. Built entirely out of wood, the palace suffers dreadfully from damp but still manages to stage performances.

Tserkov Troitsy (Church of the Trinity)
Overlooking the estate's artificial lake, the Church of the Trinity (1692) was built by a serf architect on the site of a small wooden church. Limestone decorates the five-domed brick structure whose chief glory is the intricately carved wooden iconostasis. The palace grounds to the west consist of woods and a fair.

OSTANKINSKAYA TELEBASHNYA (OSTANKINO TV TOWER)
At 540m (1,771 ft) the world's second-tallest freestanding tower after Toronto's CN tower, the Ostankino TV mast was also the scene of the most vicious gunfire during the uprising of October 1993 (note the pockmarks in the nearby

Ostankino Palace *Tel: 283 4645. Open: May to Sept, Wed–Sun 10am–6pm. Closed in damp weather. Admission charge. Metro: VDNKh, then bus or trolleybus down Ulitsa Akademika Korolyova to the lake.*

trees). Almost destroyed by fire in August 2000, it needed massive reconstruction and only reopened in 2004.

Tel: 282 2038, 282 2293. www.tvtower.ru. The administrative building is on Novomoskovskaya Ulitsa. Trolleybus 13 from metro VDNKh takes you directly there.

VVTS (ALL-RUSSIAN EXHIBITION CENTRE)

This grandiose park was formerly the Exhibition of Economic Achievements, a Soviet Disney World displaying a fantastically sanitised version of communist reality. Square-jawed proletarians stand over the monumental gates to 2sq km (³/₄sq mile) of kitsch pavilions once devoted to such Soviet staples as 'Metallurgy', 'Atomic Power', 'Education of the Peoples' and 'Grain'.

Today commercialism has taken over: in the Cosmos Pavilion, the Apollo-Soyuz docking craft have been shoved aside to accommodate a showroom of BMWs and Harley-Davidsons.

Open: (grounds) Mon–Fri 9am–7pm; Sat, Sun, holidays 9am–8pm, (pavilions) Mon–Fri 9am–6pm; Sat, Sun, holidays 9am–7pm. Free admission. Metro: VDNKh.

The lovely Ostankino Theatre, within the 18th-century palace of Count Nikolai Sheremetev

Pushkin – creator of
modern Russian literature

Squares

Each of the squares described below offers its own focus of
interest. With the exception of Red Square and Theatre
Square, site of the imposing Bolshoy Theatre, none
perhaps merits a special visit, but all of them are essential
crossroads of Moscow urban life.

Komsomlskaya Ploshchad (Komsomol Square)
'Komsomol' was the abbreviation of the
League of Young Communists, whose
members helped build the palatial
metro station beneath your feet.

Above ground, equally memorable is
the architecture of the railway termini
surrounding the square. Yaroslavskiy
Vokzal (Yaroslavl Station), start of the
grand Trans-Siberian railway (and
adjoining the Leningrad terminus), was
built in Russian fairytale style by Fyodor
Shekhtel in 1902–4, while the exuberant
Kazanskiy Vokzal (Kazan Station) is the
work of Aleksei Shchusev, better known
for designing Lenin's Mausoleum (*see p49*).

Between the stations stands the
Leningrad Hotel, one of seven 'wedding
cake' buildings constructed to Stalin's
taste in the 1940s and '50s.
Metro: Komsomolskaya.

Krasnaya Ploshchad (Red Square)
See pp40–1.

Lubyanskaya Ploshchad (Lubyanka Square)
The square is dominated by the
Lubyanka (*see p48*), nickname of
the former KGB's headquarters. To the
right is the 19th-century Polytechnic
Museum building (*see p56*), while to the
left is Russia's biggest toyshop, Detskiy
Mir (Children's World).
Metro: Lubyanka.

Ploshchad Revolyutsii (Revolution Square)
Remains of the 16th-century city walls
back the square, a favourite site of
communist demonstrations to this day.
Shining behind the walls is the cupola of
the Zaikonospasskiy Monastery (*see p70*).

The ornate red-brick City Duma
(council) building, on the left as you
leave the metro, was until recently the
grandest of the USSR's many Lenin
museums, exhibiting Lenin's works
in well over 100 languages.
Metro: Ploshchad Revolyutsii.

Pushkinskaya Ploshchad (Pushkin Square)
The elegant Strastnoy Monastery was
torn down in 1937 to make room for
this favourite Moscow meeting place at
the intersection of Tverskaya Ulitsa and
the Bulvar (*see p68*). The monument to
Pushkin, unveiled in 1880 in the
presence of writers Ivan Turgenev and
Fedor Dostoevsky, is on the western side
of the square.
Metro: Pushkinskaya, Tverskaya.

Staraya Ploshchad (Old Square)

A thriving market place in the 19th century, Staraya Ploshchad was better known more recently as the home of the Communist Party Central Committee (building No 4), ideological epicentre of the Soviet Union. Some of the area's old charm is captured in the 1694 Tserkov Vsyekh Svyatikh (Church of All Saints) at the far end of the square and the gloriously decorated Church of the Trinity on nearby Nikitnikov Pereulok (*see p71*).
Metro: Kitay Gorod.

Taganskaya Ploshchad (Taganka Square)

Much of the 19th-century anthill of artisans' dwellings, cheap hostels and taverns in this quarter was destroyed by Soviet town planners, leaving little more than a vast expanse. However, it was celebrated under communism for the barely tolerated Taganka Theatre and its favourite son, Russia's Bob Dylan, Vladimir Vysotsky, who died of drink in 1980.
Metro: Taganskaya.

Teatralnaya Ploshchad (Theatre Square)

The Bolshoy (Big) Theatre, designed in 1825 by Osip Bove, is both an architectural and cultural Moscow landmark. Rivalled only by St Petersburg's Mariinskiy (formerly Kirov) Theatre, its stage has played host to attractions as diverse as the great singer Fedor Chaliapin and the 1922 founding ceremony of the Soviet Union. (*See also pp152–3.*) It shares the square with the Children's Theatre and the Maliy (Small) Theatre, to its right and left respectively. A huge granite impression of Karl Marx looks across Teatralniy Proezd.

A ceramic frieze enlivens the outside of the luxuriously restored Metropol Hotel (one of the oldest hotels in Russia, designed in 1898 by William Walcott) to Marx's right on Teatralniy Proezd. Constructed at the turn of the last century, its *style moderne* interior is well worth a look.
Metro: Teatralnaya, Okhotniy Ryad.

Teatralnaya Square is dominated by the Bolshoy Theatre

Tretyakovskaya Galereya (Tretyakov Gallery)

The Tretyakov Gallery boasts the largest collection of Russian art in the world (some 100,000 paintings in all). It was founded by the millionaire industrialist Pavel Tretyakov who presented his private collection to the city of Moscow in 1892. The original building was designed in the Russian revivalist style by Viktor Vasnetsov and completed in 1905.

Icons are a main feature at the Tretyakovskaya

The gallery was closed in 1985 for a comprehensive programme of restoration completed in the 1990s. There is a second picture gallery, the Novaya Tretyakovskaya Galereya (known familiarly as the Tretyakovka), devoted to 20th-century art. This is on a different site entirely.

Icon Painting

Icon painting, like Christianity itself, came to Russia via Byzantium. Most of the earliest icons are from Kiev, the cradle of Russian civilisation; the oldest, the austere *Virgin of Vladimir*, located in

Old site (Tretyakov) *Lavrushinskiy Pereulok 12. Tel: 951 1362. www.tretyakov.ru. Open: 10am–7pm Tue–Sun (last admissions 6.30pm). Closed: Mon. Admission charge. Tours available in English. Metro: Tretyakovskaya.*
New site (Tretyakovka) *Krymskiy Val Ulitsa 10/14. Tel: 238 1378. Open: 10am–7.30pm Tue–Sun (last admissions 6.30pm). Closed: Mon. Admission charge. Tours available in English. Metro: Park Kultury.*

a church incorporated into the gallery's southern wing, dates from the 11th century. The early schools of Kiev, Novgorod and Pskov paved the way for artists of the naturalistic Moscow school which flourished from the 14th to 17th centuries. There are masterpieces by the great trio of Moscow iconographers: Theophanes the Greek, Dionysius and Andrei Rublev, as well as the 17th-century master, Simon Ushakov.

18th- and 19th-Century Art

The story of Russian art continues on the second floor with the European-trained painters of the Academy of Arts, founded by Catherine the Great in the 18th century. The works on show include portraits and landscapes by Dmitry Levitsky, Vladimir Borovikovskiy and Vasilu Tropinin.

In the 1870s a group of artists including Ivan Kramskoy, Vasily Perov and Fedor Vasilev rebelled against the straitjacket of academicism and went in search of a new, national art. The subject matter of these artists, who became known as the *Peredvizhniki*

(Wanderers) and went on to include Vasily Surikov, Vasily Polenov, Alexei Sarasov and the prolific Ilya Repin, ranges from portraits and vast historical canvases, through landscapes and religious paintings to vivid exposés of the horrors of war and the causes of social conflict (*see also p58*).

After The Wanderers

Within the space of a generation, the Wanderers had been overtaken by a new wave of artists including several future collaborators of Diaghilev's Ballets Russes: Valentin Serov, Alexander Benois and Konstantin Korovin.

In the 20th century Russian painters entered the vanguard of European art, with Mikhail Larionov, Natalya Goncharova and Kazimir Malevich. Their work is highly original, but there is clear evidence too of the influence of the European Cubo-Futurist school. Many of these artists, including Vasily Kandinsky, were forced to leave Russia after the Revolution because of tightening ideological constraints.

The Tretyakovka

The New Tretyakov takes over where the old one left off with artists of the early 20th century. Most of the Soviet art belongs to the Socialist Realist school which set out in the 1920s as an attempt to make art more accessible to the people, but which later degenerated into an ideological tool of the regime. What's on offer is a movable feast, but some of the more original artists to look out for include Isaak Brodsky, Aleksandr Deyneka and Sergei Gerasimov. (*See also p39.*) The second floor is devoted to temporary exhibitions by contemporary artists. (Separate charge.)

The old site of the Tretyakov Gallery

A comparatively recent addition to the attractions of Moscow, this park is certainly worth visiting. It is a little way out from the centre, but it is easily reached by metro, trolleybus or car. Dominated by its obelisk and museum, Park Pobedy covers over 9ha (22 acres) and was built to commemorate the 50th anniversary of Russian victory in the Great Patriotic War of 1941–5. To reach the museum, pass through the large Victory Square, which has a row of fountains and five marble blocks, each representing a year of struggle against Nazi Germany. After a pleasant walk, visitors reach a massive obelisk 141.8m (465ft) high – representing 10cm (4 inches) for every day Russia was at war.

Right behind the obelisk is a pair of World War II howitzers, standing by the entrance to the museum. Allow at least two hours in this immense building – even longer if you have a special interest in military history. Displays include Russian, German and even Japanese military equipment. The panoramic life-sized sets representing major battles and sieges are breathtaking. Visiting the Central Hall of Glory, containing the names of all Heroes of the Soviet Union, and the Memorial Hall – where books

name every citizen of the USSR who fell in the war – can be a deeply emotional experience.

Right next to the museum is an open-air display of World War II tanks, howitzers, trains and aeroplanes. The church of St George, Bringer of Victory, is on the main Victory Square, alongside a memorial mosque and synagogue.

Victory Park should be visited twice: once during the day to visit the museum and see newlyweds come to pay homage to the victims of war, and then at night to enjoy the warm breeze of a Moscow

evening and to see the fountains illuminated in red for the blood spilled in 1941–5. In summer, this place is busy until well past midnight with people roller-skating, strolling or just enjoying a drink.

If you happen to be in Moscow on 9 March, you can join tens of thousands of Russians here celebrating National Victory Day – the main public holiday, since every Russian has a relative who suffered in the war. Festivities in Victory Park include concerts, speeches by veterans and fireworks, and last throughout the day and late into the night.

Children may enjoy a nearby amusement park, which has numerous rides. Although Victory Park is quite new and some of it is still under construction, it has quickly become popular among Muscovites and tourists alike.

Museum open: Tue–Sun 10am–6pm.
Closed: Mon and last Thur of the month.
Metro: Park Pobedy.

Opposite above: Park Pobedy is popular among many Muscovites
Opposite below: Arch of Triumph commemorating Russian victory over Napoleon in the Battle of Borodino
Above and right: Illuminated fountains make this park even more attractive at night

W a l k :   T v e r s k a y a   U l i t s a   a n d   P a t r i a r s h i y   P r u d

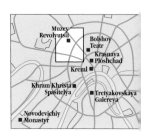

Named after the market town of Tver 150km north of Moscow, Tverskaya Ulitsa's broad expanse begins the long highway to St Petersburg. It was reconstructed as Gorky Street in the 1930s to Stalin's grandiose taste. The up-market shops demonstrate the new-found wealth of many Muscovites; the contrastingly peaceful environs are the focus of much of the capital's literary history.

Allow 2½ hours.

Begin at Mayakovskaya metro station.

1 Triumfalnaya Ploshchad (Square of Triumph)

'Comrades, to the barricades!... Streets are our brushes, squares are our palettes!' Thus exhorted the poet Vladimir Mayakovsky, the laureate of Soviet communism, whose statue dominates the square (which also used to bear his name). Behind him stands the resolutely Stalinist Peking Hotel, while to his right are Kontsertniy Zal im P I Tchaikovskovo (Tchaikovsky Concert Hall) and Teatr Satiry (Theatre of Satire).

Bear down Tverskaya Ulitsa towards the Kremlin.

2 Muzey Revolyutsii (Museum of the Revolution)

The exhibits here offer a balanced view of Russia's unsettled politics to the present day. The crumpled trolleybus in the forecourt came abreast of a tank during the abortive 1991 coup. (*See p55.*)

3 Pushkinskaya Ploshchad (Pushkin Square)

In summer amorous couples and drunks compete for benches in the shade around the statue of Russia's national poet, Alexander Pushkin, to whom the square is dedicated. For centuries a favourite meeting place, it is now the site of the world's largest McDonald's restaurant. A ferment of poets, politics and black market traders in the late 1980s, it now harbours pickpockets rather than *agents provocateurs.*

Continue down the left of the street.

4 Lower Tverskaya Ulitsa

Passing the waxworks museum at No 14 (*see p156*), the faded glory of the adjoining Yeliseev's food store is worth a look before reaching Tverskaya Ploshchad where Moscow's founder, Yuri Dolgorukiy, faces the city council building. A world-weary Lenin sits in isolation to his rear, oblivious of the reconstruction to his left of 18th-century Tserkov Cosmy i Damiana (SS Cosma

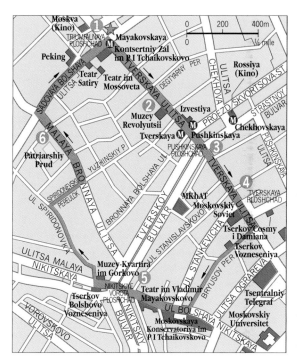

remembered in the Art Nouveau house-museum (Muzey-Kvartira im Gorkovo) at nearby Ulitsa Malaya Nikitskaya 6/2 (*see p56*). Next comes the house of poet Alexander Blok; opposite lived the officially approved writer Alexei Tolstoy, a distant relative of *the* Tolstoy. *Turn right on Ulitsa Spiridonovka then right along Spiridonevski Pereulok, then left on to Malaya Bronnaya Ulitsa.*

and Damian Church), until recently the Culture Ministry printing works.

The façades of Nos 9 and 11 across the road are built of granite earmarked by the Germans for a victory monument following the expected fall of Moscow. Through the arch gleams the cupola of the delicate Tserkov Vozneseniya (Church of the Ascension), built in 1629.

Turn into Bryusov Pereulok and then right again into Ulitsa Bolshaya Nikitskaya and away from the centre.

5 Literary Moscow

The TASS news agency stands at the corner of Ulitsa Bolshaya Nikitskaya and the Bulvar. Author Maxim Gorky is

6 Bulgakov's Moscow

When the Devil comes to torment Moscow in Mikhail Bulgakov's masterpiece *The Master and Margarita*, he makes his first appearance at the tranquil Patriarshiy Prud (Patriarch's Ponds). The novel was suppressed by Stalin and was not published until 1966. Its author died blind and penniless in 1940. Much of the action is set around the corner in apartment 50, Sadovaya Bolshaya Ulitsa 10, where Bulgakov lived in the early 1920s. The graffiti festooning the staircase bear witness to the cult-like following he enjoys to this day.

Turn right on to Sadovaya Bolshaya Ulitsa to return to Mayakovskaya.

Walk: Kitay Gorod

The financial heart of Moscow until the Revolution, Kitay Gorod is one of the longest inhabited parts of the capital and largely escaped the brutal Soviet town planning of the 1930s. Impregnable battlements and proximity to the Kremlin attracted artisans' guilds in the Middle Ages, while the concentration of wealth and strict monastic orders played their part in establishing Russia's first centre of learning.

Allow 1½ hours.

Start at metro Lubyanka and head down Teatralniy Proezd to the Nikolskiy Gates.

1 Nikolskiy Vorota (Nikolskiy Gates)

This is the last remaining of seven former gateways in the mighty walls

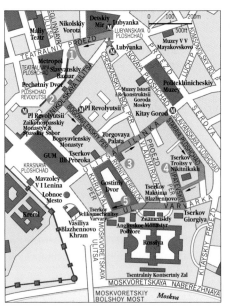

around Kitay Gorod. The name of the stronghold probably derives from the wooden laths (kiti) built into the walls for strength.

Head through the arch and turn right along Nikolskaya Ulitsa. The Slavyanskiy Bazaar restaurant at No 7 was a favourite haunt of Russian literati, including the writer Chekhov, the theatre director Stanislavsky and the composers Rimsky-Korsakov and Tchaikovsky.

2 The Russian Renaissance

An elaborate stucco façade decorates the turquoise building at No 15, erected in Russian Gothic style on the site of the former Synodal Printing House. Here in 1564 Ivan Fedorov set the type of *The Acts of the Apostles*, Russia's first book. Further down the street in the courtyard of No 9 is another crucible of the Russian Renaissance, the 17th-century Zaikonospasskiy Monastery. The greenish building at the back of the yard was the Slavic-Greek-Latin

Academy, Russia's first university.
The Spasskiy Sobor (Spasskiy
Cathedral), once one of the greatest
examples of Russian Baroque
architecture, suffered use as a dormitory
for metro engineers and a dog-lovers'
club under the Soviets.
*Retrace your steps and turn right down
Bogoyavlenskiy Pereulok.*

3 Financial Moscow

Facing you at the end of the street is the
classical portico of the former Stock
Exchange (*birzha*) building, now the
Chamber of Commerce (Torgovaya
Palata). Beside it on Ulitsa Ilinka and
Rybniy Pereulok stands what was once
the mercantile heart of Russia, the Old
Merchants' Chambers or Gostiniy
Dvor, marketplace of traders from all
over the empire.

Heading left along Ulitsa Ilinka,
note the imposing black façade of the
Ministry of Finance at No 9. No 27 is
the grandiose premises of the Northern
Insurance Society, now home to Russia's
Constitutional Court.
*Turn right along Staraya Ploshchad (see
p63), then right into Nikitnikov Pereulok
before turning right down Ipatevskiy
Pereulok.*

4 Tserkov Troitsy v Nikitnikakh
(Church of the Trinity in Nikitnikakhi)

The delicate red and white spade gables
contribute to the beauty of one of
Moscow's most celebrated churches,
completed in 1653. The frescos and
iconostasis are largely the work of the
master Simon Ushakov.
*Retrace your steps to the top of Ipatevskiy
Per and turn right on to Ulitsa Varvarka.*

The imposing bulk of Moscow's Chamber of
Commerce building on Ulitsa Ilinka

5 Ulitsa Varvarka

The hulking Rossiya Hotel (1967)
dominates this street of glorious little
churches which miraculously escaped
the demolition of a whole district prior
to the hotel's construction. At No 12 rise
the five indigo cupolas studded with
gold stars of the 17th-century Tserkov
Giorgiya (Church of St George), now a
shop selling folk arts and crafts. Next
door is the Romanov House, built by
Mikhail Romanov's grandfather (*see p54*).

The simple Tserkov Maksima
Blazhennovo (Church of St Maxim
the Blessed) stands at No 6, while the
16th-century Angliyskoe Podvore
(English Residence), donated by Ivan
the Terrible to members of the London
Muscovy Company, is at No 4a. The
street comes to an end with the pastel
exterior of the classical Tserkov
Velikomuchenitsy Varvary (Church of
St Barbara).

Stalin's Skyscrapers

Any visitor to Moscow will soon encounter a monumental, neoclassicist high-rise building, with the Soviet emblem and maybe a star on its beacon. After a day or two in Moscow, one finds this building seems to dominate the city. At this point, do not make the usual tourist mistake. Never use this building as a landmark: there are seven of them and they are almost identical!

Known as Stalin's skyscrapers, they were built in 1950–53 at the dictator's behest. Meant to commemorate 800 years of Moscow's history, in fact they represent the might of the Soviet Union in the 1950s, when it was perhaps the most powerful country in the world. The Soviet 'empire', including many satellite states, reached from the Pacific in the East to the Baltic Sea in the West. It was exporting the communist ideology across the world and the Soviet Union was gaining the upper hand in the arms and space races with the USA.

Two of these skyscrapers serve as ordinary apartment blocks, though they are anything but ordinary. They are in the city centre and the apartments are very large, so they are only for the 'more than better-off'. Visitors can sample these buildings by checking in to the Hotel Ukraine or Hotel Leningrad, the third and fourth of the series. Two more house the Ministry of Interior and the Ministry of Transport and Services, but the one that is really worth visiting is the State Lomonosov University, in Sparrow (formerly Lenin) Hills, a favourite destination for newlyweds and tourists alike. A large fountain right in front of the building emphasises its monumental size.

The construction of these buildings was under the direct supervision of one of Stalin's most feared henchmen – Lavrenty Beria, who led the feared NKVD (later KGB). In 1993, during reconstruction of his former villa, dozens of skeletons were found in his garden. He was executed soon after Stalin's death.

If the weather allows, there is a beautiful view over a very large part of Moscow, from an unusual perspective. The view is dominated by the large Luzhniki stadium, built for the 1980 Olympic Games, which were boycotted by the USA. Four years later there was no Soviet team at the Olympics held in Los Angeles.

Although these buildings contain no tourist attraction, they inspire deep nostalgia among Muscovites for the once mighty and undefeated Soviet Union, where progress was the key word. If there are three things characteristic of Moscow, they are the Kremlin, Red Square and Stalin's skyscrapers. And if you happen to visit any former communist-bloc capital such as Riga, Warsaw or Prague, do not be surprised if you see one of them there too – a present from Soviet Russia.

The might and the glory of the Soviet Union represented in one building

Walk: The Arbat

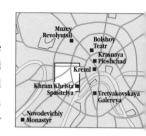

Dirty-kneed children and frock-coated merchants ... the last decades of a doomed aristocracy ... underground printing presses and impoverished artists ... this is the soul of the Arbat quarter of the city that still filters through today's pedestrian mall and souvenir shops. The grimy courtyards and twisting backstreets readily conjure up scenes of working-class life at the inception of the Revolution, while the time-worn mansions of Ulitsa Prechistenka speak of an age never to return.

Allow 2½ hours.

Start at metro Arbatskaya. Take a look at the vast Ministry of Defence (Ministerstvo Oboroniy) building behind you before crossing the road to Ulitsa Arbat.

1 Ulitsa Arbat

Alive with street musicians, beggars, snappily-dressed mafiosi and long-haired youth, the Arbat retains something of the bohemian atmosphere of days gone by. The region around the street played host at various times to such luminaries as writers Pushkin, Lermontov, Tolstoy, Gogol and Bulgakov and composers Scriabin and Rachmaninov.

The street was also a hotbed of political dissent – the basement of No 9 housed one of the country's largest anti-tsarist printing presses.

Once the main route to Russia's

Note: large parts of Arbat are under reconstruction. Works move from building to building; it is therefore difficult to say which will be next.

western lands, the Arbat was the road to Stalin's dacha in the 1930s, patrolled by a legion of secret police for whom the luxurious Praga restaurant (on the right-hand corner) was converted into a dining hall. The concentration of intelligentsia made the area a prime target of Stalin's terror, as recorded in Anatoly Rybakov's novel *Children of the Arbat* – hugely popular during the *glasnost* era. The author lived at No 51.

Make a detour left down Bolshaya Afanasevskiy Pereulok, immediately left again and then right on to Filippovskiy Pereulok.

2 Side Streets

As you make your way along the Arbat, duck into as many of the courtyards and side streets as you can: each has its own fascination. Spasopeskovskaya Ploshchadka 36, where Scriabin used to give concerts, is a wonderful example of the Russian carved *izba* (wooden cottage). Further along, Krivoarbatskiy Pereulok 10 was the home of the modernist architect Konstantin Melnikov, dubbed 'the Russian Le Corbusier', whose genius was ultimately snuffed out by Stalin – for 40 years, until his death in 1974, not one of Melnikov's projects was realised. To the right up Spasopeskovskiy Pereulok is the residence of US Ambassadors to Russia, Spaso House, built in 1914 for the financier Nikolai Vtorov (later murdered by a Red Army guard). Return to Ulitsa Arbat then go left down Plotnikov Pereulok. Wander south through the embassies of one of the city's most fashionable residential districts until you come to Ulitsa Prechistenka, the aristocratic stronghold of old Moscow. No 12 is now Literaturniy Muzey A S Pushkina, a museum devoted to the poet Pushkin, while No 11, Muzey L N Tolstovo, is dedicated to Tolstoy (*see p57*).

3 Khram Khrista Spasitelya

Until 1934, this was the site of the vast Cathedral of Christ the Saviour whose dome dominated the city skyline. It was blown up to make way for what was to have been the world's largest building, Stalin's Palace of Soviets. Inexplicably, the foundations continuously flooded, and Khrushchev abandoned the project, digging out a swimming pool (Basseyn Moskva) instead. The unsanitary state of the pool forced city authorities to close it in 1993. Work began on a replica of the old cathedral and it was consecrated in 1999. Today all major religious services are held here (*see pp36–7*) and the cathedral contains a museum. *Museum Khrama Khrista Spasitelya, Volkhonka 15. Tel: 202 8024. Open: daily 10am–6pm, except Mon. Free admission. Metro: Kropotkinskaya.*

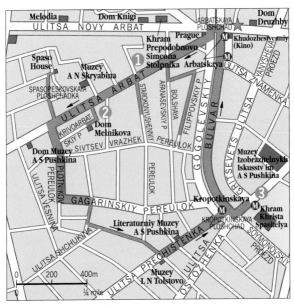

Walk: Kuznetskiy Most and the Neglinnaya

A little of the 19th-century exclusivity of Kuznetskiy Most is being reborn in brightly lit shop windows, while the backstreets giving on to the Bulvar reach deep into Moscow's medieval past.

Allow 1½ hours, excluding visits to the steam baths and circus.

Head straight for Kuznetskiy Most from the metro station of the same name.

1 The Neglinnaya River

Kuznetskiy Most – Smiths' Bridge – is named after the metalworkers in the cannon foundry established on the left bank of the Neglinnaya River by Ivan the Terrible. Though the bridge was dismantled when the river was enclosed underground, its name lived on in the city's centre of finance and fashion. The jeweller Fabergé displayed his marvels in today's 'Rifle' clothing shop, No 21/25 was the headquarters of the first Russian Insurance Society, while around the corner at Neglinnaya Ulitsa 12 stands the Central Bank of the Russian Federation.

Continue right along Neglinnaya Ulitsa, then turn right into Neglinnaya Pereulok.

2 Sandunovskiye Banyi (Sandunovskiy Baths)

Much loved by Moscow's literati – the author Chekhov had a private room overlooking No 2 – the historic steam baths at Neglinnaya Pereulok 14 are worth a look. The interior, with its carved oak cubicles, stained glass and elegant light fittings dating from the early 19th century, breathes faded grandeur. (*For details on Russian 'banya' procedures, see p158.*)

Turn left at the end of Neglinnaya Pereulok on to Ulitsa Rozhdestvenka.

3 To Stretenskiy Monastyr

The 18th-century country house to the left with the prettily tiled façade is Moscow's Architectural Institute, and Tserkov Nikolaya v Zvonaryakh (Church of St Nicholas in Zvonaryakh) next door, named after the Kremlin bellringers who lived nearby, houses the institute's drawing school.

Turning right down Bolshoy Kiselny Pereulok and left on to Ulitsa Lubyanka Bolshaya, you reach the remains of the Stretenskiy Monastery, founded in 1395. Built in honour of the miraculous icon which came to Tamerlane in a dream and dissuaded him from attacking Moscow, the cathedral and its glorious frescos are now under restoration following years of abuse when it was used as a club for members of the KGB.

4 Rozhdestvenskiy Bulvar and Monastyr

The most elegant of the capital's boulevards begins with the tiny chapel of Our Lady Most Holy, attached to a church occupied by a derelict naval museum. Opposite on Stretenskiy Bulvar a statue to Lenin's wife, Nadezhda Krupskaya, stands in place of the Stretenskiy Gates – pulled down by Stalin in the 1930s.

The far left corner of Rozhdestvenskiy Bulvar is the site of an ancient convent, constructed in 1386 on the upper banks of the Neglinnaya River. Although the convent was closed soon after the Revolution, two old nuns, Varvara and Viktorina, continued to live there until the former was strangled by an icon-smuggler in 1978. The convent has now reopened.

Enjoy the view over the rooftops from the end of the boulevard and walk down to the square.

5 Trubnaya Ploshchad and Tsvetnoy Bulvar

Trubnaya Ploshchad used to be the site of bustling livestock and bird markets. On Annunciation Day (25 March), Muscovites traditionally bought birds and released them into the air – profitable business for the traders who trained them to return for subsequent resale. Neighbouring Tsvetnoy Bulvar was the city's main flower market but is now loved for the Tsirk (State Circus – *see p157*) on the left. See *www.circusnikulin.ru* for contact details and opening times. *Tsvetnoy Bulvar metro station is just beyond the circus.*

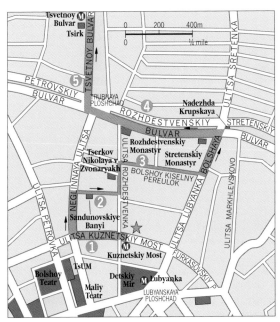

Walk: Kutuzovskiy Prospekt and Park Pobedy

Kutuzovskiy Prospekt is a long, wide boulevard very typical of Moscow. Named after the famous Marshal Kutuzov, it links various sites connected to Russian victories.

Allow 1½ hours excluding visits to museums.

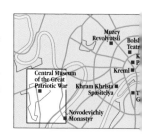

Start at Park Pobedy metro and head down Kutuzovskiy Prospekt towards the Arch of Triumph.

1 Museum and Panorama of the Battle of Borodino

As well as original and replica artefacts connected with the Napoleonic invasion, there is a huge panorama here depicting scenes from the Battle of Borodino in 1812. Although the heydays of panoramas are past, this one is remarkable: 115m (377ft) long and 15m (49ft) high, the painting includes about 3,000 figures. Behind the museum is a replica of the hut where Marshal Kutuzov took the momentous decision to abandon Moscow before the advancing Napoleonic army (*for opening times see p54*).

Cross Kutuzovskiy Prospekt and retrace your steps to reach Victory Square.

2 Victory Square

This large square dominates *Park Pobedy* (Victory Park). It is a favourite destination at weekends, and numerous benches next to large fountains offer a relaxing place to enjoy your drink or snack bought at one of the nearby food stands. While walking through the square, notice the five marble blocks, each representing a year of war between 1941 and 1945.

Walk through the square towards the church on the left.

3 Church of St George, bringer of Victory

The church was built in the 1990s to commemorate all victims of World War II in the Soviet Union. It is a small but beautiful church with the characteristic golden cupola and rich interior. The nearby memorial mosque and synagogue may also be visited.

Proceed through the square towards the museum.

4 Central Museum of the Great Patriotic War

This monumental museum holds a large display of World War II military artefacts and two beautiful memorial halls. At least two hours are needed to see it properly. The museum building is semicircular, supported by numerous pillars and dominated by a large dome. The impression of might is reinforced by the obelisk over 100m (328 ft) tall in front of the museum. The designer Zurab Tsereteli finalised plans for the project in 1995. (*For more details of the museum, see pp66–7.*)

On leaving the museum, turn right and proceed down the steps.

Beautiful 'flower clock' on one of the slopes in Victory Park

5 Exhibition of Military Technology

The tanks, howitzers, planes and other military hardware here are all original and some are rare, such as the armoured battle trains. Visitors may see things from a soldier's point of view in the trenches by walking through a front-line military installation. There are German and Russian planes of the 1940s, but also more recent Russian fighter jets and helicopters. The display is open only in good weather.
Central Museum of Great Patriotic War and the Exhibition of Military Technology. Open: Tue–Fri 10am–5pm. Closed: last Thur of month.

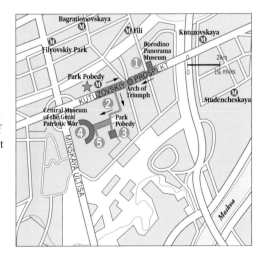

Speaking of Russia, one of the first things that comes to mind is vodka. It is indeed the national drink. No celebration, party or even Sunday lunch is complete without it. Russian vodka is good and relatively cheap, but its popularity has caused much hardship among Russians over the years. The abuse of vodka still creates serious problems and even led to prohibition under Gorbachev.

But prohibition merely gave rise to an illicit trade in alcohol, while others turned to home-brewed *samogon*, which caused many deaths from alcohol poisoning. The ban on alcohol did not solve or improve anything. Fortunately, in recent years increasing numbers of Russians have started to turn away from hard liquor and lead a more healthy life.

Besides being *the* vodka country, Russia is becoming famous for its many kinds of beer (*pivo*). Their quality can easily compete with other European brands. Russia's cheap labour force has attracted foreign breweries from the USA, the Netherlands and even South Africa. Every shop in Russia boasts at least 20 brands of Russian or foreign beer. In summer, restaurant gardens are packed with Muscovites enjoying their beer with the obligatory dried fish, called *vobla* or *taranka*. Some Russians even drink 'yorsh' – a beer and vodka cocktail! By the way, it is quite normal in Russia to walk around the city while drinking beer straight from the bottle.

There are other characteristic drinks enjoyed by Russians that are alcohol-free. Tea is important in everyday life. 'Russian tea' is always drunk black and it is made with only a small amount of water, so it is very strong. This potent extract is poured into individual tea cups and each drinker dilutes it to taste with boiling water. Sugar is not placed in the tea, but either bitten off a large sugar lump, or placed in the mouth and the tea drunk through it. While enjoying their tea, Russians like to munch on something, such as red or black caviar on bread and butter – or chocolate.

Another favourite drink is *kvas*, which is a bread-based, sweet beverage – rather like beer, but non-alcoholic. It is quite filling and Russians drink it with *pirozhki* (savoury doughnuts) or *blini* (pancakes). *Pirozhki* are filled with mince, mushroom, cabbage or a fruit marmalade. They really match the sweet and slightly heavy taste of *kvas*.

Russians are very hospitable, so if you are ever invited to a Russian home, be prepared: you will be expected to eat and drink large quantities. The unprepared stomach may suffer from overload and nothing calms it better than the typical Russian sour milk called *kefir*.

Would you like some Russian, Czech, German, Dutch, Austrian or any other beer?

Walk: From Khram Khrista Spasitelya to Gorki Park

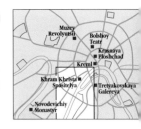

Near the Kremlin and Red Square, this route gives an interesting and different view of Moscow's centre and includes museums, parks and a church.

Allow about 2 hours excluding visits to museums.

Start at Kropotkinskaya metro, right in front of Khram Khrista Spasitelya.

1 Khram Khrista Spasitelya (Cathedral of Christ the Saviour)

This is the largest church in Moscow and a dominant feature on its skyline. Consecrated in January 2000 (it was built for Moscow's 850th anniversary), it proudly stands on its hill above the river, a replica of the original church that stood here until the communist regime tore it down. All major religious celebrations are held here, attended by thousands of believers. The interior exactly duplicates the original, with some additions. Despite the old style of architecture, the church was built using the latest materials and modern construction methods.

(*For more details of the Cathedral of Christ the Saviour, see pp36–7.*) Cross the street and walk towards the centre, to Ulitsa Volkhonka.

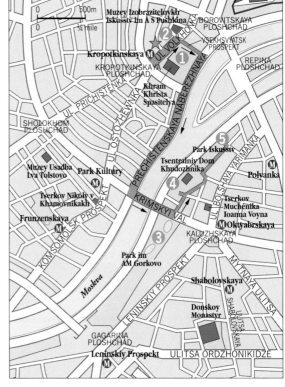

2 Muzey Izobrazitelnykh Iskusstv im A S Pushkina (Pushkin Fine Arts Museum)

One of the best-known art museums in Moscow, this was built at the end of the 19th century and start of the 20th century. It includes art and artefacts from ancient Egypt, but is better known for its collection of European art, with paintings by Botticelli, Rembrandt and Canaletto, Italian art of the 14th to 18th centuries, as well as impressionists, post-impressionists and modernists such as Cézanne, Gauguin, Van Gogh, Picasso and many others (*see p38*).

Head down Vsekhsvyatsk Prospekt to the river, turn right and proceed along the embankment (Prechistenskaya Naberezhnaya Street), past the memorial statue dedicated to Peter I, until you reach the first bridge, then cross the river; or you can take the metro to Oktyabrskaya station.

3 Park im A M Gorkovo (Gorki Park)

A well-known favourite (even before the film of the same name!), Gorki Park stands on the banks of the Moskva River, a relaxing retreat from the hectic city centre. You can stroll through this large park, or simply relax in the shade or on numerous benches. Children enjoy the many rides in the local amusement park, but Gorki Park is certainly not just for children. It is a venue for regular concerts and many student celebrations. If you ever become tired of the pulsing city around you, visit Gorki Park for a wonderful and relaxing afternoon. *Open: daily summer 10am–10pm; winter 10am–9pm. Admission charge.*
Cross the bridge approach road (Krimskyi Val) and follow the small street opposite.

4 Tsentralniy Dom Khudozhnika (Central Artists' House)

The Central Artists' House was built in the 1970s for an exhibition of Soviet art. This project did not materialise and the building became the Central Artists' House instead. Part of it houses a branch of the Tretyakov Gallery with a permanent exhibition of 'Art of the 20th Century' (*see p39*).
Continue through the grounds.

5 Park Iskusstv (Arts Park)

The grounds of the Central Artists' House became a resting place for many colossal statues of communist politicians and artists. After the fall of the regime, their prominent display on pedestals no longer seemed appropriate. It is quite odd to walk through this pleasant park looking at figures who were once among the most powerful in the world. Arts Park is also a good place to buy paintings.

Luna Park rides and attractions in Gorki Park are enjoyed by both the young and the old

Walk: From Lubyanka to Manezhnaya Ploshchad

Sometimes overlooked, this route between Kitay Gorod and the centre runs from the old headquarters of communist oppression to the new one of free trade. Those with good legs or those short of time may make it one long walk from Kitay Gorod to Gorki Park.

Allow 1½ hours for this walk excluding visits to shopping centres or the Manezh.

Start at Lubyanka metro.

1 Lubyanka
The large building on Lubyanskaya Square, by the architect Aleksandr

Shchusev, is known simply as Lubyanka – a name feared by Russians. Rumour suggests Lubyanka is as big below ground as above. The headquarters of the notorious KGB had a jail, death row and possibly torture chambers, for those who dared oppose the communist regime. Many who entered it were never seen again, and many more were sent to labour camps in Siberia – a sentence equal to death, since few returned alive.

Until 1991 a statue of Felix Derzhinskiy, founder of the NKVD (the KGB's predecessor), stood on the pedestal in front of the building, but is now in the Arts Park (*see p83*). Lubyanka today belongs to the FSB, successor of the KGB in the democratic state. *Proceed down towards the centre, along Teatralniy Proezd Street, until you reach the large Teatralnaya Ploshchad.*

2 Teatralnaya Ploshchad
On this square stands one of the world's best-known theatres, the

Fountains on Manezhnaya Ploshchad provide a welcome place to cool down on a hot summer's day

3 Okhotniy Ryad

Once an area of small town houses, this is now one of the most highly commercial parts of Moscow. Notable buildings are the Russian Duma (lower house of Parliament) and the Hotel National. Okhotniy Ryad is better known for its three-level shopping centre. Opened in 1997, it offers boutiques, fast-food outlets, Internet cafés, sports bars and even casinos. Its cupola showing the northern hemisphere merges well with the fountains in the square above.

4 Manezhnaya Ploshchad

The foot of this square is dominated by the Hotel Moscow and it reaches to the Manezh exhibition hall opposite – hence its name, Manezhnaya Ploshchad. The arena, built in 1817 for the visit of Alexander I, blends simplicity with monumentality. After the tsar's visit, it was used as the Imperial Riding School. Today it is the venue for national and international exhibitions, well worth visiting. Its floor area of 6,500sq m (70,000 sq ft), almost as big as Christ the Saviour Cathedral, is truly astonishing.

Bolshoy, one of the largest in Europe and famous for its opera and ballet performances. It is also a fine example of Russian 19th-century architecture, designed by O I Bove and A A Mikhailov (*more details on pp152–3*).

Teatralnaya Ploshchad has fountains by which to cool off in the summer months, and two more theatres – the Children's and the Small Theatre. Also interesting is the Hotel Metropol, built in the early 20th century in modernist style and well worth a look inside.

Opposite the Bolshoy is a statue of Karl Marx, whom communists see as the founder of communism and socialism. This is one of the last communist-era statues in the city on its original spot, and die-hard communists still meet here. *Continue in the same direction to Okhotniy Ryad and Manezhnaya Ploshchad.*

The square did not exist until the 1930s. It runs alongside the Alexsandrovsky Sad, at the heart of the centre, close to the Kremlin, Red Square and Tverskaya Street. The square is always full of adults chatting and relaxing on its benches, children drawn to its many fountains, and in summer people enjoying a walk until the early hours. Visitors to Moscow tend to fall in love with this square and keep coming back to it.

Walk: Zamoskvoreche

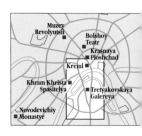

Translating as 'Beyond the Moscow River', this area was the city's wild frontier in the Middle Ages, a densely forested region manned by isolated Cossack outposts on the main highway to the settlements of the dreaded Tartar Khans. Subsequently, Moscow's gentry chose Zamoskvoreche for their city estates, and the wealth of classical mansions and graceful churches ideally complements a visit to the main attraction, the Tretyakov Gallery.

Allow 2 hours, excluding the Tretyakov Gallery.

Start from Oktyabrskaya metro.

1 Kaluzhskaya Ploshchad (formerly October Square)

A colossal statue of Lenin dominates this square. Moving down Ulitsa Bolshaya Yakimanka (to Lenin's right), note the fanciful French Embassy, built at the turn of the 20th century in a pastiche Old Russian style. Opposite rise the chequered cupolas of Tserkov Muchenika Ioanna Voyna (Church of St John the Warrior), a breathtaking example of early 18th-century religious architecture.

Turn right down Khvostov Pereulok to Ulitsa Bolshaya Polyanka.

2 Ulitsa Bolshaya Polyanka

Facing you as you join Ulitsa Bolshaya Polyanka is the 1695 Tserkov Uspeniya (Church of the Dormition). Down the street

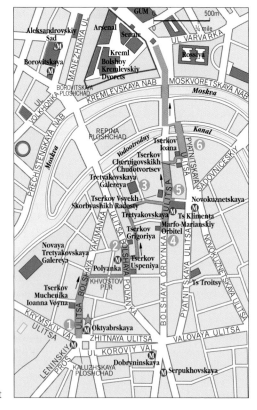

at No 29a is the attractive Tserkov Grigoriya (Church of St Gregory), a wonderful multicoloured confection dating from the 17th century.

Retrace your steps 50m (55yds) and turn down peaceful Staromonetniy Pereulok, taking the second right into Bolshoy Tolmachevskiy Pereulok.

3 Around the Tretyakovskaya

On the right of the street at No 3 stands one of Moscow's finest classical mansions, built in 1770 for the fantastically wealthy Siberian mining magnate Demidov. On the left is the Church of St Nicholas, now part of the Tretyakov Gallery (*see pp64–5*).

Walk ahead to Bolshaya Ordynka Ulitsa and head right to No 34.

4 Marfo-Marianskiy Obitel (Convent of SS Martha and Mary)

Assisted by the greatest contemporary artists, Grand Duchess Yelizaveta Fedorovna founded this convent in 1908 after her husband Sergei, the governor of Moscow, was blown up by a revolutionary's bomb. The Church of the Virgin's Veil was built in the ancient Novgorod style by A V Shchusev, who went on to design Lenin's mausoleum (*see p49*). The grand duchess's cells house the laundry of a hospital now occupying the grounds. She herself was executed with the rest of the royal family in 1918.

Return towards the centre along Bolshaya Ordynka Ulitsa.

5 Bolshaya Ordynka Ulitsa

In the 14th century this was the chief road along which the Tartar horde invaded Moscow demanding tribute and slaves. The churches and pre-Revolutionary estates make for a rare tranquillity. Note especially the Baroque masterpiece Tserkov Klimenta (Church of St Clement, to the right down Klimentovskiy Pereulok) and Tserkov Vsyekh Skorbyashikh Radosty (Church of the Joy of All who Sorrow), funded in 1834 by the merchant Dolgov who lived in the mansion opposite.

Cut down Chernigovskiy Pereulok.

6 To the Kremlin

On the right you come to the small stone Tserkov Chernigovskikh Chudotvortsev (Church of the Chernigov Miracle Workers), after which the lane is named, and to the left the ensemble of Tserkov Ioana (Church of St John). Turning left on to well-preserved Pyatnitskaya Ulitsa, note on the right-hand corner the restored headquarters of the original Smirnoff vodka company – the words read 'Supplier to his Imperial Majesty, Pyotr Arsenyevich Smirnov'. A battle is now raging between the original Smirnovs and the US-owned distillers over lucrative rights to the family name.

Cross the bridge to continue towards the Kremlin.

Church of St John the Warrior

Excursions from Moscow

Once you get tired of the busy city life in Moscow and decide to get away from it all and breathe some fresh air, do not be afraid to go on some short excursions. This is a good opportunity to visit the countryside and experience a different kind of Russia. Quiet walks through the country will give you the opportunity to meet a more relaxed people than the always busy and rushing Muscovites. Trips to the country may be undertaken on your own or alternatively you can contact local excursion bureaux.

Opportunities to stock up with souvenirs are aplenty

Abramtsevo

This tranquil country estate, set among woods and ponds, is best known as the retreat of a group of artists, 'The Wanderers' (*see p58*). The railway magnate and impresario Savva Mamontov bought the house and grounds in 1870; under his patronage painters such as Ilya Repin, Mikhail Vrubel and Viktor Vasnetsov produced some of their finest work.

The Church of Our Saviour among the trees is the result of collaboration by the artists: Vasily Polenov designed the beautiful iconostasis while the icon of the Saviour is the work of Repin. Mamontov is buried in the adjoining chapel. *Reach by elektrichka (80 minutes) from Yaroslavskiy Vokzal, or drive down Yaroslavskoye Shosse towards Sergiev Posad until signpost to Abramtsevo. Tel: 8 254 32470. Open: Wed–Sun 10am–5pm. Closed: last Fri of the month. Admission charge.*

Borodino

Over 100,000 troops died in one day in 1812 on Russia's most famous battlefield, now a vast museum-reserve littered with memorials of Napoleon's plans to capture Moscow. Mass graves and trenches remain elsewhere about the site, testament to the 1941 bitter engagement at Borodino during World War II.

A dramatic re-enactment of the Napoleonic battle, complete with bayonet charges and cavalry, takes place yearly on the weekend nearest 7 September (details from museum). *Borodino is 124km (77 miles) from Moscow. Take elektrichka from Belorusskiy Vokzal and walk 3km (2 miles) from Borodino station to the museum. By car, take Minskoye Shosse to Mozhaisk; Borodino village is 12km (7¹/₂ miles) west. Tel: 8 238 51057. Museum open: 10am–6pm. Closed: Mon and last Fri of the month. Admission charge.*

Gorki Leninskie

In the heyday of Soviet power, half a million visitors a year paid homage at the estate where Lenin died, aged 53, in January 1924 after a series of strokes.

Clocks in the estate are stopped at 6.50, the time of his death, and though the premises are falling into disrepair, some curios remain.

Gorki Leninskie is 35km (22 miles) south of Moscow. Take elektrichka from Paveletskiy Vokzal then bus 27 or 28. Alternatively, join a Patriarshy Dom Tour (tel: 795 0927). By car take Kashirskoye Shosse. Tel: 548 9309. Open: 10am–4pm. Closed: Tue and last Mon of the month. Admission charge.

Marfino

This peaceful village north of Moscow harbours the remains of an estate belonging to Peter the Great's tutor, Prince Golitsyn. The estate has been spoilt by conversion into a Soviet workers' pension, but the picturesque lakeside setting makes for a superior summer picnic spot.

Take elektrichka from Savyolovskiy Vokzal to Katuar station (40 minutes), then catch bus 37 to estate gates. By car, drive down Dmitrovskoye Shosse until Marfino signpost.

Melikhovo

Anton Chekhov (1860–1904) wrote his ground-breaking play *The Seagull* and many of his short stories at his country estate here. The modest estate is a little barren in winter but its wild gardens are enchanting in summer or when the surrounding meadows burst with bluebells in early spring.

The buildings have been carefully preserved to capture the writer's life at the turn of the 20th century.

Melikhovo is 60km (37 miles) south of Moscow. Take elektrichka from Kurskiy Vokzal to Chekhov, then bus 25. By car, drive down Varshavskoye Shosse towards Tula till sign for Melikhovo. Chekhov

estate, tel: 8 272 24079. Open: Wed–Sun 10am–4pm. Closed: last Fri of month.

Peredelkino

This little village is best known as the Soviet Union's writers' colony where the politically correct were rewarded with luxurious country retreats. Its most famous resident was author and poet Boris Pasternak (1890–1960).

Pasternak's house is now a museum and his nearby grave is still smothered in bouquets from a grateful nation.

Peredelkino is 25km (15¹/₂ miles) west of Moscow. Reach by elektrichka from Kievskaya Vokzal, or by road via Kutuzovskiy Prospekt and Minskoye Shosse until left turn at the 21km (13 miles) post. Pasternak's house open: Thur–Sun 10am–4pm. Admission charge.

Sergiev Posad

Formerly known as Zagorsk, this town is focused around one of Orthodox Russia's key sites, the magnificent Troitse-Sergievskaya Lavra (St Sergius Trinity Monastery). Dress should be modest; tourists now take a definite second place to pilgrims and seminary students.

The monastery was founded in the 14th century by Russia's patron saint, Sergius of Radonezh, who was instrumental in organising resistance to the Tartar occupation of Muscovy. Its eerie Trinity Cathedral, with icons by Andrey Rublyov, holds a permanent service to the saint.

Sergiev Posad is 75km (46¹/₂ miles) north of Moscow. Reached by elektrichka from Yaroslavskiy Vokzal (1¹/₂ hours) or by car via Yaroslavskoye Shosse. Monastery open: 10am–6pm. Closed: Mon and weekends. Admission charge.

Zolotoe Koltso

Zolotoe Koltso (the Golden Ring) is the name of a series of medieval towns at the very heart of Russian history. Following the decline of the great Kievan state, each became a separate principality and trading centre before the Tartar invasions and eventual absorption by Muscovy.

Experience country life in Zolotoe Koltso

The main towns remain some of the best preserved and most memorable destinations of any trip to Russia – the impregnable kremlins, exquisite churches and congested markets evoke the essence of the country's feudal past. Many tours to Moscow include one or more in their itinerary. All of the towns described below (except perhaps Yaroslavl) make for a sensible day trip. Good hotel accommodation is available, often inside the monasteries. Detailed handbooks to the region are freely available in Moscow.

Rostov Veliki

'Rostov the Great' was founded on the shores of Ozero Nero (Lake Nero) as early as the 9th century and is famed for its outstanding fortress, or kremlin, built in the late 1600s. Within its walls are several gloriously decorated churches; outside, the Uspenskaya Tserkov (Church of the Assumption) steals the scene, while a number of ancient monasteries are within easy reach of the town centre.

Suzdal

Suzdal is the true gem of the Golden Ring, a sleepy rural town 220km (137 miles) from Moscow, packed with picturesque churches and rickety wooden cottages about the slow-moving Kamenka River. At its zenith, Suzdal boasted over 70 churches and monasteries, many donated by merchants grown rich on the city's fertile land. Even those daunted by the prospect of more onion domes and icons will be delighted by perhaps Russia's most beautiful tourist attraction.

Vladimir

Once Russia's capital, the ancient city of Vladimir is now a grubby textile and defence industry centre 180km (112 miles) east of Moscow. Today the city is racked by the modern evils of unemployment and pollution, but its glorious past as the headquarters of Russia's medieval strongman Yuri Dolgorukiy is still reflected in a number of architectural masterpieces. The 1158 Uspenskiy Sobor (Cathedral of the Assumption) on the heights above the river was the model for its namesake in the Moscow Kremlin and housed the revered Vladimir Mother of God icon, now displayed in the Tretyakov Gallery (*see p64*). Vladimir also holds probably the last remaining example of old Russian military architecture – the Golden Gate built in the early 12th century.

There are many historic sites in towns around Moscow

Yaroslavl

In 2010, Yaroslavl will celebrate the 1,000th anniversary of its founding. Founded as a trading post on the Volga River, Yaroslavl is the largest of the Golden Ring cities. Like its neighbours, it was ransacked by the Tartars but emerged as a flourishing princedom hosting English and Dutch traders travelling to Moscow from Archangelsk on the White Sea. Fortified monasteries and the lavish 17th-century Tserkov Ioana Zlatousta (Church of St John Chrysostom) recall its former days of mercantile splendour.

If you are an ice-hockey fan, make sure you visit a home game of the local Torpedo Yaroslavl ice hockey team, which is amongst the best in the Russian league. Its line-up contains some former NHL stars as well as some Russian national team members.

Zvenigorod

The hilltop city of Zvenigorod was founded at the end of the 13th century in what is known as the 'Russian Switzerland', a lovely landscape at its best as the leaves turn with the onset of winter.

On the road heading out of town, note the remains of the old city kremlin, climbing from the Moskva River. A footpath leads to the graceful Uspenskaya Tserkov (Church of the Assumption, 1396) on top of the hill. A little further up the road lies the magnificent white-stone Savvino-Strozhevskiy monastery. It was closed down in 1919, but restoration is fast resurrecting the gatehouse church and the monastery cathedral. Andrey Rublyov, greatest of Russia's icon masters, decorated the cathedral, and in 1918 three of his original icons were discovered in a woodshed on the hilltop. They are now on view in Moscow's Tretyakov Gallery (*see pp64–5*). *Zvenigorod is 90 minutes by elektrichka from Belorusskiy Vokzal or one hour by car along Uspenskoye Shosse. Monastery open: 10am–5pm. Closed: Mon. Admission charge.*

A short ride on a suburban train leaves behind the city's emerging sophistication and takes the traveller back in time to an entirely different world – the Russian countryside.

Vast expanses of farmland, isolated cottages huddled under the severe northern sky, and headscarved women sitting beneath brightly decorated window frames watching strangers with a wary eye is a picture that changes little the length and breadth of Russia.

The almost idyllic scenes often conceal a life of extreme hardship.

The stoicism of the Russian *muzhik* – peasant – is legendary, facing changes in politics and the weather with the same dour patience. The older among them vividly remember the terror and famines of one of Stalin's most senseless policies, collectivisation, from which country life is only now beginning to recover.

Historians reckon that 14 million were killed in the 1930s, either by starvation, firing squad or in exile, as a result of the forcible destruction of private farming to create gigantic collective farms and communist 'agrotowns'. Wealthy

peasants, dubbed *kulaki* or 'tight fists', were singled out for special treatment: 'We must smash the kulaks, eliminate them as a class,' Stalin ordered.

Those who resisted were sent to labour camps in Siberia or shot in their villages. Stealing one ear of corn was classified as robbing the state and punishable by up to ten years' imprisonment. One boy, Pavlik Morozov, who denounced his father for hoarding grain, was held aloft as an example to Soviet children. Streets are still named after him in Moscow.

For all its suffering, the village community is still at the heart of the Russian nation. Before the Revolution, 90 per cent of the population lived in the country. Most of today's city-dwellers are only two or three generations removed from the fields – perhaps accounting for the popular saying that Moscow is 'just one big village'.

The peacefulness and beauty of the Russian countryside will allow you to refresh yourself for your next trip

Sankt Peterburg (St Petersburg)

Saint Petersburg, cultural capital of Russia, was founded in 1703, when Peter the Great snatched a soldier's bayonet and cut a cross in the soggy turf of an island in the Neva River. He probably did not say 'Here a city begins!' because at first he planned just a fort and harbour. Only later did he add a town.

St Petersburg's coat of arms

Now the streets are granite, the palaces are marble, Peter's equestrian statue is bronze and the city is on the tourist

BRIDGE OPENING TIMES

When travelling at night, keep in mind the times when bridges over the Neva are opened to let shipping through (*see below*). If you get stuck, your only hope is to bargain with a boatman to ferry you across.

Most Alexandra Nevskego *02.20–05.05*
Birzhevoy Most *02.10–04.50*
Volodarskiy Most *02.00–03.45, 04.15–05.45*
Grenaderskiy Most *02.45–03.45, 04.20–04.50*
Dvortsoviy Most *01.35–02.55, 03.15–04.50*
Kantemirovskiy Most *02.45–03.45, 04.20–04.50*
Leytenanta Shmidta Most *01.40–04.55*
Liteiniy Most *01.50–04.40*
Petra Velikogo Most (Bolsheohtinskiy) *02.00–05.00*
Sampsonievskiy Most *02.10–02.45, 03.20–04.25*
Troitskiy Most *01.50–04.50*
Tuchkov Most *02.10–03.05, 03.35–04.45*

map. For years the city was neglected in favour of Moscow, but, for its 300th anniversary, President Vladimir Putin has relaunched his home town. That has not come cheaply. About £1 billion has been spent repainting, restoring and reopening the western portal of the Mosque, rooms in the Russian Academy of Sciences, the Mikhaylovsky garden, the Hermitage entrance from Palace Square and rooms of the *Pushkinsky dom.*

St Petersburg celebrated its 300th anniversary in 2003 with laser shows, an aqua-bike show, a regatta on the Neva, gala concerts, a daytime firework display, multicoloured balloons, an international festival of military brass bands and a rock concert, as well as a 50-hour dance marathon.

President Putin gave a warm welcome to the EU leaders who gathered in St Petersburg for the EU–Russia summit in the Konstantinovsky Palace in Strelna.

The Politics of a Name

During World War I, the city's name was changed to the less Germanic 'Petrograd'. In 1924 the Bolsheviks renamed it 'Leningrad'. The name 'St Petersburg' was readopted by referendum in 1991 when

St Petersburg Town Plan

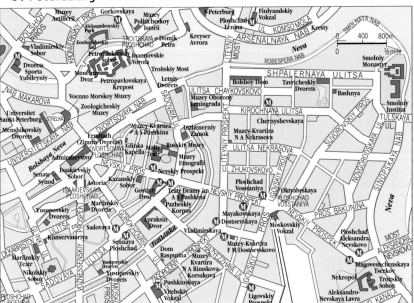

the flush of anti-Soviet enthusiasm was at its most passionate, but many of its five million inhabitants continue to call the city Leningrad.

ALEKSANDRO-NEVSKAYA LAVRA (ALEXANDER NEVSKY MONASTERY)

The monastery was founded by Peter the Great, supposedly on the site of Prince Alexander Nevsky's 1240 victory over the Swedes. Today, the peeling paintwork of official neglect and crows fluttering above the graveyards combine to leave a haunting impression.

Blagoveshchenskaya Tserkov (Cathedral of the Annunciation)

Designed by Peter's chief builder Domenico Trezzini, this church once

served as the Romanovs' necropolis and still contains the tombs of Russia's greatest military mind, General Aleksandr Suvorov (1730–1800) and Catherine the Great's leading statesman, Prince Aleksandr Golitsyn. The adjoining red-and-white monastery buildings, fine examples of Petrine architecture, are occupied by the city blood donation centre and are closed to the public.

Cemeteries

A gateway in the right-hand wall of the drive leads to the Tikhvinskoe Kladbishche (Tikhvin Cemetery), containing the graves of some of Russia's greatest artists, including the writer Fedor Dostoevsky and the composers Modest Mussorgsky and

General view of SS Peter and Paul Fortress

Nikolay Rimsky-Korsakov. In the far right corner, a harrowing bust captures the exhausted soul of Pyotr Ilych Tchaikovsky who committed suicide in 1893.

Opposite, the Lazarus cemetery is the resting place of the aristocracy but also contains the graves of the polymath Mikhail Lomonosov, Pushkin's wife Natalia Goncharova and many of the city's architects.

Troitskiy Sobor (Cathedral of the Trinity)

Catherine the Great's taste for classicism created a headache for the architect Ivan Starov. Yet he succeeded – the vast interior (1790), for all its ornamentation, retains an Orthodox intimacy. The remains of Alexander Nevsky, canonised by the church, lie in a sarcophagus to the right of the iconostasis. (As this is a working church, women should cover their heads.)

Ploshchad Aleksandra Nevskovo. Tel: 274 0409. Monastery open: dawn–dusk. Free admission. Tikhvin Cemetery open: Apr–Oct 9.30am–8pm, Nov–Mar 9.30am–4pm. Lazarus museums and exhibitions open: Apr–Oct 9.30am–6.30pm, Nov–Mar 9.30am–4pm. Closed Thur. Admission charge. Metro: Ploshchad Aleksandra Nevskovo.

KREYSER *AVRORA* (CRUISER *AURORA*)

A blank shot from the bow cannon of this tiny warship gave the signal for Red Guards to take the Winter Palace in October 1917 (*see pp14–15*), sealing the fate of the Provisional Government and securing the *Aurora* an almost legendary status in Soviet revolutionary history.

Floating Museum

Today you are free to wander around the immaculately preserved ship, inspect the cannon and take a look at the radio room. A mock-up of sailing conditions – the ship's menu records that Baltic Fleet sailors enjoyed 123g of vodka and salt cabbage daily – is on display below decks. The museum also shows off the red flag which was raised on the night of the Revolution, as well as period uniforms and weaponry, songs composed in the ship's honour and gifts from various foreign communist dignitaries dating from the heyday of Soviet Bloc bonhomie. Today the *Aurora* is maintained by cadets from the nearby Nakhimov Navy School.

Petrogradskaya Naberezhnaya 4. Tel: 230 8440. Open: Tue–Thur, Sat–Sun 10.30am–4pm. Free admission. Metro: Gorkovskaya.

PETROPAVLOVSKAYA KREPOST (PETER-AND-PAUL FORTRESS)

The fortress was designed to protect the Neva lands won from the Swedes during the Northern War (1700–21). The founding of the fortress on 16 May 1703 is considered to mark the founding of the city itself.

The fortress was first built in wood and later rebuilt in stone by Domenico Trezzini. One island was chosen as a construction site, at the point where the river branches into three arms: the Bolshaya ('Big') Nevka, Neva and Malaya ('Small') Nevka. The name of the fortress was soon transferred to the city.

Museums and Exhibitions

The Komendantskiy Domik (Commandant's House) and Inzhenerniy Korpus (Engineer's House) display exhibitions of city history. You can also visit the Boathouse (Botny Domik) and the Mint.
Across the river from Winter Palace. Tel: 238 0505. Open: Mon, Thur–Sun 11am–6pm; Tue 11am–5pm. Closed: Wed and last Tue of month. Metro: Gorkovskaya.

Petropavlovskiy Sobor (Cathedral of SS Peter and Paul)

The cathedral is a unique example of Russian 18th-century architecture. The first, wooden, church dedicated to Sts Peter and Paul was begun in 1703. It took 21 years to build this cathedral designed by Trezzini. For two centuries it was the burial place of Russian emperors. All the tsars and grand dukes of the Romanov family were buried here including Nicholas II, laid to rest in 1998, 80 years after their execution in Ekaterinburg.

Trubetskoy Bastion

From 1872 to 1921 the cells in the bastion served as a prison. From the late 18th century the fortress was a gaol for Russian revolutionaries. Reading and writing were outlawed and total isolation was enforced: guards were forbidden to speak or to know the identity of inmates and patrolled soundproofed corridors. Insubordination meant the *kartser* or cooler (literally – it was unheated in winter); mere rudeness to the guards merited two days' darkness. Today, it is open to visitors.
Open daily 10am–7pm.

PETER THE GREAT (1672–1725)

Fired by travels abroad in his youth, Peter modelled his court on Versailles, streamlined the bureaucracy and championed industrialisation. But despite his passion for reason in a country steeped in superstition, Peter had a strong streak of the barbarian in him. Soirées at the Summer Palace dissolved into gothic debauchery. St Petersburg was constructed, much as Stalin's projects were, by sheer effort of will and drastic loss of life. Capable of extreme cruelty, Peter personally saw to the torture of Alexei, his only son. Like Gorbachev, Peter was adored by westernisers but was similarly motivated less by love of the 'effete' West than by the need to make the Russian system work better, remarking: 'We shall need Europe for a few decades and then we can show her our backside!'

Waterways

One of the world's most beautiful maritime cities, St Petersburg is defined by the River Neva, which gave the city its first harbour. It was built to open Russia to sea trade with Northwest Europe. The first ship sailed up the Neva in November 1703. Tsar Peter was so overjoyed that he rowed out to pilot it in personally, before buying the whole cargo of wine and salt. He gave the captain 500 gold roubles and, when the Dutchman explained that he was bound for the Swedish port of Narva, Peter offered him another 300 roubles to return promptly.

The Neva's south bank is drained by a series of concentric canals and rivers. At times the elements proved too much for them. Catherine the Great awoke on the morning of the great flood of 1777 to be told that her wing of the Winter Palace was about to be submerged.

The waterways offer enchanting views of St Petersburg – often called 'the Venice of the North' because this unique city is built on 44 islands, linked by over 600 bridges. During the shipping season, from 19 April until 30 September, various boat trips allow you to see palaces, churches, monuments, gardens and bridges effortlessly. The trips vary from 40 minutes to 1 hour and cost about 300 roubles.

Below: Fontanka Canal
Right: Griboyedova Canal

Dvortsovaya Ploshchad (Palace Square)

The footsteps of Imperial Guards and revolutionary detachments no longer echo across the square, yet this stage on which the drama of Russian history has played still readily conjures up its restless past.

Palace Square and Alexander Column

Enclosed by the Winter Palace and the General Staff building, Palace Square was the tsars' favourite military parade ground. It was also the epicentre of the revolutions that condemned the Romanovs to what Trotsky contemptuously referred to as 'the rubbish bin of history'.

The 1905 Revolution began on 'Bloody Sunday', when a crowd marched on the square petitioning Nicholas II to improve living and working conditions. Hundreds were killed when guards opened fire on the peaceful demonstrators, fatally wounding the weak tsar's image as the people's 'Beloved Father'.

On 25 October 1917, night of the Bolshevik Revolution, the square was the scene of the capture of the Winter Palace by Red Guards under Trotsky's command (*see pp14–15*). Their aim was the arrest of the Provisional Government, unsuccessfully defended by 300 Cossacks.

The American journalist John Reed asked an opposition politician whether the insurrection would succeed: 'The devil knows!' he replied. 'Well, perhaps the Bolsheviks can

The wonderful façade of the Winter Palace

seize power, but they won't be able to hold it more than three days ... Perhaps it's a good thing to let them try – that will finish them ...'

Today the square is a favourite venue for political meetings and popular entertainment.

Aleksandrovskaya Kolonna (Alexander Column)

The Alexander Column in the centre of the square is dedicated to Tsar Alexander I for his role in the triumph over Napoleon. The inscription on this monument to the defeat of Napoleon reads: 'To Alexander the First from a Grateful Russia.' The column was designed by Auguste de Montferrand in 1829. It took over a year to haul the 600 tonne (590 ton) monolith, at 47.5m (156ft) high the largest of its kind in the world, from a Finnish quarry to St Petersburg. Over 2,000 soldiers and war veterans, cheered on by a huge crowd and watched by Nicholas I, pulled it on to the pedestal where it remains. Thanks to the original system of scaffoldings and winches, developed by the French engineer Betancourt, it took only two hours to lift the column on to the pedestal. It is not fastened to its foundation; due to accurate calculations, it is held in its place by its own weight.

Glavnyi Shtab (General Staff building)

To the south, Palace Square is bounded by a grand building, built to house the General Staff and the ministries of foreign affairs and finance. These enormous edifices are united by a monumental arch spanning Bolshaya Morskaya Street.

It was not easy to arrange the 600m (1,969ft) façade – then the longest in Europe – in such a simple and expressive way. Carlo Rossi (1775–1849) skilfully solved the task, accentuating the central part by a majestic arch, conceived as a monument to the Patriotic War of 1812. The arch is decorated with armour and flying glories and topped with Victory driving a six-horse chariot. Today it houses the Hermitage museum.

Zimniy Dvorets (Winter Palace)

The tsars' stunning winter residence, the fourth Winter Palace, was completed by Bartolomeo Rastrelli in 1762. After 1881 Alexander III moved to Gatchina and the Winter Palace was used only on especially solemn occasions. For a few months in 1917 the palace was the home of the Provisional Government. It is considered the masterpiece of Russian Baroque architecture, created, in Rastrelli's own words, 'exclusively to glorify Russia'.

Most of the interior, apart from the elegant Jordan Staircase, has been remodelled since Rastrelli's time according to the whim of passing tsars. The palace was almost entirely burnt to the ground in the fire of December 1837 but was completely rebuilt by Easter 1839.

Its staggeringly opulent state rooms and halls now function as what is probably the world's most luxurious art gallery (*pp102–5*).
Metro: Nevskiy Prospekt, then trolleybus 1, 7 or 10 or taxi-bus.

Ermitazh (State Hermitage Museum)

This is one of the world's truly great art museums. Among the Hermitage's treasures are art works by Leonardo da Vinci, Raphael, Titian, Rembrandt and Rubens, a celebrated collection of impressionist and post-impressionist paintings, not to mention work by Matisse and Picasso. World-renowned are the collections of Scythian gold and the antiquities from the shores of the Black Sea.

The New Hermitage building

The story of the Hermitage begins with Peter the Great who brought back paintings from foreign tours and showed them in his Kunstkammer (*see p110*). But it was during the reign of Catherine the Great that the collection really took shape. In 1764 she received 225 works from the Berlin merchant Gotzkowsky, who had made the collection for the Prussian King, Frederick II, who, owing to reverses in the Seven Years War, had to put the collection up for sale. The collections of Baron de Thiers and the British prime minister, Sir Robert Walpole, which she also acquired, included large numbers of European masters.

Catherine allowed only selected guests to view the works, and it was not until the October Revolution of 1917 that the doors of the Hermitage opened to the people. After the Revolution, many private collections were added to the Imperial one. As a specified German target, the museum's treasures were evacuated to the Urals during World War II. Today the Hermitage museum comprises six buildings: the Little Hermitage, the Old (Large) Hermitage, the New Hermitage, the Hermitage Theatre, part of the General Staff Building and the Winter Palace. *Dvortsovaya Naberezhnaya 34. Tel: 710 9625. www.hermitagemuseum.org. Open: 10.30am–6pm; Sun 10.30am–5pm. Closed: Mon. Admission charge. Free on Thur for individuals. Tours available in English. Metro: Nevskiy Prospekt, then trolleybus 1, 7 or 10, or taxi-bus.*

Viewing the Collection

To spend just one minute looking at each of the exhibits would take over 12 years, so a visit should be planned carefully to avoid severe picture fatigue. The box opposite outlines the main order of the exhibition which occupies the former Winter Palace (entered through the chief Neva embankment entrance) and the Small and Large Hermitages.

The Golden Rooms

It has taken over two centuries to assemble the unique collection of gold, silver and gems fashioned into fascinating pieces of jewellery by

Russian, European and Oriental artists and craftsmen.

The gold of the Nomads is represented by unique finds from the north coast of the Black Sea, the northern Caucases and western Siberia. Greek gold from the shores of the Black Sea is featured in the exhibition. The jewellery art of the East and of South America is unknown to most people and very rare.

Temporary Exhibitions
The Hermitage hosts temporary exhibitions, advertised in the foyer.

The State Rooms
The State Rooms of the tsars' Winter Palace are a breathtaking display of Imperial elegance. The Main Staircase, left from the ticket offices, leads majestically to the Antechamber, Nicholas Hall and Concert Hall before you arrive at the Malachite Room (189) where the Provisional Government convened before they were ousted by the Bolsheviks in the 1917 Revolution.

Alternatively, turn right at the top of the staircase and head through the Field Marshall's Hall to Peter's Throne Room and the Armorial Hall. A door to the left leads to the 1812 Corridor, lined with paintings of the field commanders who defeated Napoleon, and through to the magnificent St George's Hall (198), adorned with a mosaic map of the USSR set with semi-precious stones.

Prehistory and Antiquity
Occupying much of the ground floor, the Hermitage's collection includes a number of Egyptian mummies and sarcophagi and a display of classical

KEY TO ROOMS

Ground Floor
11–33 Prehistory
55–69 Central Asia and Russian Far East
100 Ancient Egypt
101–31 Classical Antiquity

First Floor
147–53, 157–87 Russian art and culture
155–6, 188, 197, 204, 260, 271, 282, 289, 304–7 State rooms
207–38 Italian art, 13th- to 18th-century
239–40 Spanish art, 15th- to 19th-century
245, 247, 249–54 Dutch and Flemish art, 15th- to 17th-century
263–8 German art, 15th- to 18th-century
272–5, 278–97 French art, 15th- to 18th-century
298–301 English art, 17th- to 19th-century

Second Floor
314–30, 343–50 French art, 19th- to 20th-century
333–42 European art, 19th- to 20th-century
351–69, 383–93 Middle and Far Eastern art
398–400 Numismatics (coins and medals)

artefacts – delicate cameos, terracotta figurines, mosaics, fine statuary, etc.

Russian Art and Culture
The collection consists of over 300,000 items and reflects a 1,000-year Russian history. This section is devoted mostly to icons, ceramics and furniture, old books and archaeological finds that represent the inner world and way of life of ancient Russia. (Russian painting is

largely confined to the Russian Museum
– *see pp106–7.*)

Highlights of the Picture Gallery
Among the countless paintings, look out
for the following delights listed below.

Italian
*Madonna and Child with Sts Dominic
and Thomas Aquinas* by Fra Angelico,
room 209.
Madonna with a Flower and *Madonna
and Child* by Leonardo da Vinci,
room 214.
Danae and *The Repentant Mary
Magdalene* by Titian, room 221.
Lamentation by Paolo Veronese, room 222.
Madonna Conestabile by Raphael,
room 229.

Spanish
The Apostles Peter and Paul by El Greco,
room 240.
The Luncheon by Diego Velázquez,
room 239.
Portrait of Antonia Zarate by Francisco
de Goya, room 239.

Dutch and Flemish
*Perseus and Andromeda, Feast at
the House of Simon the Pharisee* and
Bacchus by Peter Paul Rubens,
room 247.
Portrait of Charles I and *Virgin with
Partridges* by Anthony Van Dyck,
room 246.
Danae, Abraham Sacrificing Isaac and
The Return of the Prodigal Son by
Rembrandt, room 254.

General view of Palace Square

French

Tancred and Erminia and *Landscape with Polyphemus* by Nicolas Poussin, room 279.

The Stolen Kiss by Jean-Honoré Fragonard, room 288.

English

The Infant Heracles Killing Snakes by Joshua Reynolds, room 300.

Portrait of a Lady in Blue by Thomas Gainsborough, room 298.

Modern European Art

Do not miss the wonderful collection of impressionist and post-impressionist works, and the canvases by Picasso and Matisse. The latter were acquired from the collections of two Russian philanthropists, Ivan Morozov and Sergey Shchukin, who kept the artists solvent early in their careers.

Woman Holding a Fruit by Paul Gauguin, room 316.

The Lilac Bush and *Cottages* by Vincent Van Gogh, room 317.

Still Life with Curtain and *The Smoker* by Paul Cézanne, room 318.

A Lady in a Garden and *Waterloo Bridge: Effect of Fog* by Claude Monet, room 319.

Portrait of the Actress Jeanne Samary by Auguste Renoir, room 320.

Woman Combing her Hair by Edgar Degas, room 326.

The Dance and *The Red Room* by Henri Matisse, rooms 344–5.

The Absinthe Drinker and *Sisters* by Pablo Picasso, room 348.

Russkiy Muzey (Russian Museum)

St Petersburg's superb collection of Russian art is comparable only with the Tretyakov Gallery in Moscow in quality and scale (*see pp64–5*). The Russian Museum's rooms provide a journey through the development of painting in Russia, from the earliest iconography to the avant-garde explosion and subsequent Stalinist orthodoxy of the 20th century.

The great colonnade of Michael's Palace

Iconography

Starting with Russia's earliest art form, icon painting, rooms 1–3 on the first floor have fine examples. One of the oldest is the 12th-century Archangel Gabriel, known as *The Angel with the Golden Hair* – the angel's stylised features reflect Byzantine influences.

Other highlights include the mid-14th-century icon of the murdered sons of Prince Vladimir, Sts Boris and Gleb, a stunning 15th-century rendition of St George fighting the Dragon, with scenes from his life, and works by the master of the genre, Andrey Rublyov.

Panoramic view of Michael's Palace

Art under Peter the Great

Russian art reached a watershed during the reign of Peter the Great. Thrilled by what he had seen in Western Europe, he sent promising artists abroad on scholarships to perfect their skills. Ivan Nikitin's *Portrait of the Hetman* (*c*1720) in room 5 and *Self-portrait with the Artist's Wife* (1729) by Andrei Matveev in room 6 illustrate the resulting break with medieval styles.

Academy of Arts

Founded in 1757, the Academy of Arts promoted classicism, emphasising subjects from history, the Bible and classical mythology. Room 9 shows an early history painting, *Vladimir and Rogneda* (1770) by Anton Losenko, depicting the horror of a Polovtsian princess after the murder of her father and brothers by her determined suitor, Prince Vladimir.

Leaps of progress in portraiture can be seen in room 10 with the work of Dmitri Levitsky, especially his canvases of *Count Vorontsov* (1780s) and academy director *Alexander Kokorinov* (1769).

Of the early 19th-century classical paintings, outstanding are Kark Bryullov's monumental *Last Day of Pompeii* (1833) and Ivan Aivazovsky's *The Ninth Wave* in room 14. Room 15 includes *The Appearance of Christ before the People* (1857), the greatest work of the academy's other hero, Alexander Ivanov.

Peredvizhniki (The Wanderers)

The group of realist artists dubbed *Peredvizhniki* was led by Ivan Kramskoy (1837–87), whose piercing portraits fill room 25. The artists set up the Association of Travelling Art Exhibitions, and came to be known as The Wanderers or Itinerants. Nikolai Ge scandalised society with the realism of his *Last Supper* (1863) in room 26. Ilya Repin is one of Russia's best-loved painters and many of his works are hung in rooms 33–5: two of the most famous are *Barge-haulers on the Volga* (1873) and the hilarious *Zaporozhe Cossacks* (1891).

Turning the Century

Russian art experienced an explosion of styles at the turn of the last century. Isaak Levitan's wistful landscapes in room 44 demonstrate his mastery of impressionism. Philip Maliavin's *Two Girls* in room 47 is considered to be one of his best works.

In the adjoining Benois wing, look out for other major 19th- and 20th-century artists including Mikhail Vrubel in room 66, Leon Bakst (room 68), Pavel Kuznetsov (room 74) and Vasily Kandinsky (room 79).
The Michael's Palace, Inzhenernaya ulitsa 2. Tel: 595 4248, 314 3448. www.rusmuseum.ru/eng. Open: daily 10am–5pm, Mon 10am–4pm. Closed Tue. Admission charge. Metro: Gostiniy Dvor. Entrance to the Benois Wing is from the Griboyedova Canal embankment.

Michael's (Engineer's) Castle

Isaakievskaya Ploshchad (St Isaac's) Square

Begun in the 1730s, this was the last of the central squares to take shape in St Petersburg.

St Isaac's Cathedral

Astoria Hotel

One of St Petersburg's leading hotels was designed by F Lidval in 1910–12 in Art-Nouveau style. Hitler had planned a banquet in the hotel, but his dreams of conquest did not come true. From 1987 to 1991 the Astoria underwent major refurbishment whilst staying faithful to the original style of the building.

The Blue Bridge (Siniy Most)

This is the broadest in the city – only 35m (115ft) span but 99.9m (328ft) wide. The first wooden drawbridge was built in 1737.

The tower of St Isaac's Cathedral dominates the skyline

Isaakievskiy Sobor (St Isaac's Cathedral)

Monument to imperial self-confidence, the imposing bulk of St Isaac's Cathedral rises majestically on the St Petersburg skyline, its grand dome visible from far out in the Gulf of Finland.

The cathedral is named after the patron saint of the Romanov dynasty, St Isaac of Dalmatia, whose feast day coincides with Peter the Great's birthday. Peter was married in the city's first St Isaac's, a small wooden church constructed near the Admiralty (Admiralteystvo). The current cathedral is the fourth version, begun in 1818 by order of Alexander I following the defeat of the French.

Auguste de Montferrand

The building was the life's work of a little-known French architect, Auguste de Montferrand (1786–1858). Having moved to St Petersburg after service in Napoleon's army, he was the unlikely winner of the competition to redesign St Isaac's. His relative inexperience made him easy prey to the authoritarian tastes of Nicholas I expressed in the final product. The tsar declined his widow's request that the architect be buried in the cathedral, but a small bust of Montferrand, together with his original models, is on display in the nave.

Imperial Splendour

St Isaac's impresses less by its design, which is architecturally uninspired, than by sheer mass and wealth of decoration. By the time it was completed in 1858, construction of the cathedral over 40 years had consumed more than 23 million roubles. Red granite was transported from Finland for the columns, while the porticos were topped with dramatic bronze reliefs. Inside, over 200kg (440lb) of gold went into gilding, white marble and lapis lazuli created a unique iconostasis, and the greatest artists of the day were commissioned to paint the interior frescos.

Climbing the 262 steps to the colonnade affords a breathtaking panorama over St Petersburg's rooftops and the Neva beyond (separate ticket required).

Isaakievskaya Ploshchad 1. Tel: 315 9732. Open: 11am–6pm (colonnade till 5pm). Closed: Wed. Admission charge. Metro: Nevskiy Prospekt then trolleybus 22 or taxi-bus K312.

St Isaac's Square

Mariinskiy Palace

Manège

The former Horse Guards Riding School was constructed in 1804–7 by the architect G Quarenghi. On both sides of the portico are sculptures representing the Dioscur brothers, crafted in marble. They were made in Italy by P Triscorni and delivered in 1817. The building is now the Central Exhibition Hall.

Mariinskiy Dvorets (Mariinskiy Palace)

It was built for Nicholas I's daughter, Grand Duchess Maria Nikolayevna, between 1839–44 by the architect A Stakenschneider. It is now the City Legislative Council.

The Monument to Nicholas I

Erected in the centre of the square in 1856–9, it was designed by the architect A de Montferrand and the sculptor P Klodt. The equestrian statue has only two points of support.

Museums

St Petersburg is often called a 'city of museums'. Its history, and even the history of Russia, is well preserved in the city's 50 plus museums. Any inquisitive person will find out everything about Russian history from the wealth of information within St Petersburg's museums.

Part of the Soviet armoury that menaced the West during the Cold War

Etnographicheskiy Muzey (Ethnographic Museum)
The exhibits illustrate the everyday life and culture of the people of Russia from the 18th–20th centuries. There are over half a million exhibits.
Inzhenernaya Ulitsa 4/1. Tel: 313 4421. www.ethnomuseum.ru. Open: Tue–Sun 10.30am–5pm. Closed: Mon and last Fri of month. Admission charge. Metro: Nevskiy Prospekt.

Kreyser Avrora (Cruiser *Aurora*)
A battleship of the Imperial Russian Navy at a permanent mooring. The exhibition illustrates the *Aurora*'s participation in the Tsushima battle of the Russo–Japanese War of 1904–5, as well as its revolutionary activities in the beginning of the 20th century and its participation in World War II.
Petrogradskaya nab. Tel: 230 8440. Open: 10.30am–4pm. Closed Mon, Fri. Metro: Gorkovskaya.

Muzey Antropologii i Etnografii (Museum of Anthropology and Ethnography)
The highlight of this museum is Peter the Great's collection of curiosities (also known as the Kunstkammer), one of St Petersburg's oldest sights. Thankfully no longer offering live exhibits, it contains pickled mutants, both human and animal, which caught the tsar's fancy and for which he paid handsomely. Bottled Siamese twins, hairy babies and two-faced embryos are displayed alongside selected vital organs.
Universitetskaya Naberezhnaya 3. Tel: 328 1412. www.kunstkammer.ru. Open: Tue–Sun 11am–5.45pm. Closed: Mon and last Wed of the month. Admission charge. Metro: Nevskiy Prospekt, Vasileostrovskaya.

Muzey Politicheskoy Istorii Rossii (Museum of Political History of Russia)
On display are original objects, documents and photographs showing Russian history of the 19th and 20th centuries including Lenin's office as in July 1917. There is also an exhibition on the life story of an outstanding Russian ballet dancer, Matilda Kshesinskaya (1872–1971), former owner of the mansion.
2/4 Kuybisheva ul. Tel: 233 7052. Open: 10am–6pm. Closed: Thur. Metro: Gorkovskaya.

Muzey Zheleznodorozhnovo Transporta (Museum of Railway Transport)
One of the oldest technical museums in the country, illustrating the history of

railway transport in Russia from the beginning. Some machines are still in working order.
Sadovaya ul 50. Tel: 315 1476. Open: 11am–5pm. Closed: Fri, Sat and last Thur of month. Admission charge. Metro: Sadovaya, Sennaya Ploshchad.

Stroganovskiy Dvorets (Stroganovskiy Palace)

This Baroque palace was designed in 1752–4 by B Rastrelli. The Stroganovs were noted collectors of everything from Egyptian antiquities and Roman coins to icons and old masters.

The building now belongs to the Russian Museum and has a display of porcelain. Also on show here is a collection of waxworks of historical figures.
Nevskiy Pl 17. Tel: 117 2360/8238. Open: Wed–Sun 10am–5pm; Mon 10am–4pm. Closed: Tue. Metro: Gostiniy Dvor.

Voenno-Istoricheskiy Muzey Artillerii, Inzhenernyh Voysk i Voysk Svyazi (Military-Historical Museum of Artillery, Engineers and Signal Corps)

Housed in the old Arsenal is the world's largest martial museum, founded in 1703,

The Military-Historical Museum of Artillery, Engineers and Signal Corps

with over 750,000 items including armaments, military uniforms, banners, orders and battle relics of the Russian Army. An open-air display features war machines and weaponry.
7 Alexandrorskiy Park. Tel: 232 0296. Open: 11am–6pm. Closed: Sun, Mon, Tue and last Thur of month. Metro: Gorkovskaya.

Voenno Morskoy Muzey (Naval Museum)

Located in the historical premises of the former Stock Exchange, designed by the architect I de Thomon in the early 19th century is the world's largest naval museum, founded in 1708. It has over 800,000 items, including dioramas and intricate models of ships of the Russian fleet. Do not miss Peter the Great's *botik*, the tiny rowing boat, also known as the 'Grandfather of the Russian Navy', in which Peter the Great learned to sail.
Birzhevaya Ploshchad 4. Tel: 328 2501/2701. www.museum.navy.ru. Open: Wed–Sun 11am–5.15pm. Closed: Mon, Tue and last Thur of month. Admission charge. Metro: Nevskiy Prospekt, Vasileostrovskaya.

Zoologicheskiy Muzey (Zoological Museum)

With over 17 million species, 500,000 of them on display, the museum is one of the finest of its kind in the world. The exhibits include a set of stuffed animals and a world-famous collection of mammoths.
Universitetskaya Naberezhnaya 1. Tel: 328 0112. Open: 11am–5pm. Closed: Fri. Admission charge. Metro: Nevskiy Prospekt, Vasileostrovskaya.

Art St Petersburg

St Petersburg is known as the cultural capital of Russia. Many outstanding architects, composers, poets and writers lived here and created their masterpieces. One of them was Alexander Pushkin, the great Russian poet, whose statue is in the centre of the Arts Square.

A monument to Alexander Pushkin

Literaturno-Memorialnyi Muzey Anny Ahmatovoy (Fontanny Dom) (Anna Akhmatova Museum (Fontanny Dom))

Dedicated to the life and work of the famous poet (*see p48*), this is the apartment where she lived from 1924 to 1952.

Nab reki Fontanki 34 (a wing of the Sheremetyevskiy Palace). Tel: 272 2211. www.akhmatova.spb.ru. Open: 10.30am–5.30pm. Closed: Mon and last Wed of month. Metro: Gostiniy Dvor.

Literaturno-Memorialnyi Muzey P M Dostoyevskogo (Fyodor Dostoevsky Literary and Memorial Museum)

The original interior of the writer's last apartment is furnished with his documents, photographs and personal belongings.

5/2 Kuznechnyy Per. Tel: 311 4031. www.md.spb.ru. Open: 11am–6pm. Closed: Mon and last Wed of month. Metro: Vladimirskaya, Dostoevskaya.

Muzey-Kvartira A S Pushkina (Alexander Pushkin Apartment Museum)

The last residence of the poetic genius, this is where he died on 29 January 1837, after his duel with Baron d'Anthès (an ardent admirer of his wife). Original books and artefacts, personal belongings and the original furnishings are on show.

Nab reki Moiki 12. Tel: 314 0006. www.museumpushkin.ru. Open: 11am–5pm. Closed: Tue and last Fri of month. Metro: Gostiniy Dvor.

The Mariinskiy Theatre

Muzey Muziki v Sheremetyevskom Dvortse (Fontannom Dome) (Museum of Music in Sheremetiev Palace (Fontanny Dom))

This 18th-century building by the architect S Cherakinskiy belonged to Count Sheremetevs. In the gala halls are items from the family's collections. Among them are objects of decorative and applied art of the 17th to 20th centuries. The St Petersburg collection of musical instruments (3,000 items) includes ones made by celebrated craftsmen or played by famous musicians, also historical rarities. In the White Hall, symphonic, choral and chamber music concerts are held. *Nab reki Fontanki 34 (next to Akhmatova Museum). Tel: 272 4411. Open: noon–6pm. Closed: Mon, Tue and last Wed of month. Metro: Mayakovskaya, Gostiniy Dvor.*

Muzey Teatralnovo i Muzycalnovo Iskusstva (Museum of Theatre and Music)

The museum is in the old city, in a building which belongs to the Aleksandrinsky Theatre. This masterpiece was built by the great architect Carlo Rossi. In 1918 it was decided to organise the first theatre museum in St Petersburg here. Its archive was based on the private collections of celebrated actors. The museum offers various tours and lectures, audio- and video-concerts and meetings with outstanding actors. *6 Pl Ostrovskogo. www.theatremuseum.ru. Tel: 311 2195. Open: 11am–6pm; Wed 1–7pm. Closed: Tue and last Fri of month. Metro: Gostiniy Dvor.*

Rimsky-Korsakov conservatory, the oldest music school in Russia

Muzey V V Nabokova (Nabokov Museum)

This is where the famous writer was born and grew up, in a distinctly privileged environment (he was driven to school in the family Rolls-Royce). The author of *Lolita* is commemorated in the personal effects and original furnishings of the house. *Bolshaya Morskaya 47. Tel: 315 4713. www.nabokovmuseum.org. Open: Tue–Fri 11am–5pm; Sat–Sun noon–5pm. Closed: Mon. Admission charge.*

Churches and Temples

In St Petersburg you will find Russian Orthodox, Roman Catholic, Armenian and Lutheran churches, a Buddhist temple, a synagogue and a mosque. The main avenue of the city, Nevskiy Prospekt, was once known as the 'Street of Tolerance', referring to the clutch of churches of different denominations which were established here in the late 18th and early 19th centuries.

Detail of decoration over the door to the mosque

Andreevskiy Sobor (St Andrew's Cathedral)

This Baroque cathedral was built by the architect A Viestt in 1764–80. Andrey Pervozvanniy is the patron saint of Russia, whose naval vessels all have flags with his cross. The Order named after him is the highest award of the Russian Federation.
6-ya liniya 11. Metro: Vasileostrovskaya.

Armyanskaya Tserkov (Armenian Church)

A Classical building built in 1771–80 by Yu Velten.
Nevskiy Prospekt 40–42.
Metro: Nevskiy Prospekt.

Buddiiskiy Khram (Buddhist Temple)

This, the first Buddhist temple in Europe, dates from 1913. The temple belongs to Russia's indigenous Buddhists, the Buryat tribe of Siberia, and is fully functional.
Primorskiy Prospekt 91.
Metro: Staraya Derevnya.

Khram Spasa na Krovi (Church on the Spilled Blood)

Only recently restored to its former glory, the church was built on the site where

Tsar Alexander II was assassinated in 1881 (hence 'on the Spilled Blood'). Unusually, the design is not neo-classical, as elsewhere in St Petersburg, but old Russian. After admiring the stunning mosaics and coats of arms on the exterior, be prepared to be bowled over by the interior décor, the work of Viktor Vasnetsov, Mikhail Nesterov and others.
Griboyedova naberezhnaya 2a. Metro: Nevskiy Prospekt.

The beautiful Mosque

Lyuteranskaya Tserkov Svaytogo Petra (Lutheran Church of St Peter)

Dating from 1832–8, this is by the architect A Briullov in a Classical style.
Nevskiy Prospekt 22–24.
Metro: Nevskiy Prospekt.

Metchet (Mosque)

One of Europe's largest and most beautiful mosques, it was opened in 1913.
Kronverkskiy Prospekt. Metro: Gorkovskaya.

Nikolskiy Morskoy Sobor (St Nicholas' Naval Cathedral)

Designed by Savva Chevakinskiy in a Baroque style, this was built in 1753–62 for sailors and Admiralty employees, and named after Saint Nicholas, patron saint of sailors. It contains two churches: the lower church for daily services and the upper church, used mainly on Sundays and for special occasions and weddings.
Nikolskaya ploshchad 1–3.
Metro: Sadovaya.

Rimsko-Katolicheskaya Tserkov Svyatoy Ekaterini (Roman Catholic Church of St Catherine)

Built in 1763–83 by Vallin de la Mothe, in a mixture of Baroque and Neo-Classical styles.
Nevskiy Prospekt 32–34.
Metro: Nevskiy Prospekt.

Sinagoga (Synagogue)

Alexander II authorised construction of the synagogue in 1869. Be prepared to purchase a skullcap on entrance.
Lermontovskiy Prospekt 2.
Metro: Sadovaya.

Sobor Kazanskoy Bogomateri (Cathedral of Our Lady of Kazan)

In a Classical style modelled on St Peter's Cathedral in Rome, this was built in 1801–11 by the architect Andrey Voronikhin on the site of a small church that housed the ancient icon of Our Lady of Kazan, hence the name. It is the main Orthodox cathedral of St Petersburg and is one of the grandest churches in the city.
Kazanskaya Ploshchad 2.
Metro: Nevskiy Prospekt.

Sobor Vladimirskoy Bogomateri (Cathedral of Our Lady of Vladimir)

This was built in 1760–1831 to the designs of P A Trezini and A A Melnikov.
Vladimirskiy Prospekt 20.
Metro: Vladimirskaya.

St Nicholas' Naval Cathedral

The Siege

For everyone living in St Petersburg, the Siege (*Blokada*) of Leningrad is an important part of their heritage; for older generations it brings terrible memories. The most tragic period in the city's history was full of suffering and heroism.

The Monument to the Heroic Defenders of Leningrad

Hitler hoped to capture the city in September 1941. His command even printed invitations to a banquet at Leningrad's Astoria Hotel. It never took place.

On 22 June 1941 the Soviet Union was attacked by Nazi Germany. Less than two and a half months later, German troops were approaching Leningrad and outflanked the Red Army. By 8 September 1941 the Germans encircled Leningrad and the siege began. It lasted for 872 days.

The lives of Leningrad's citizens became a permanent struggle against fire, bombs, cold and hunger while working to defend the city, assist the injured and take care of children and elderly people. Food and fuel stocks were very limited. All public transport stopped. But the 2,887,000 civilians (including about 400,000 children) plus troops did not even consider surrender.

The unusually cold winter of 1941–2 was the biggest test, with temperatures below –30°C (–86°F). In January 1942 there were no electricity or water supplies and the daily food ration sank to 125g (about 4^1/2oz) of bread per day. In January and February 1942, 200,000 people died in Leningrad of cold and starvation. But some military production continued and the city did not surrender.

Several hundred thousand people were evacuated across Lake Ladoga via the famous 'Road of Life' – the only route out of the besieged city. In summer, people were ferried across; in winter, lorries drove across the frozen lake under constant enemy bombardment.

In January 1943 the siege was broken, and a year later, on 27 January 1944, it was fully lifted. At least 641,000 people (perhaps 800,000) had died. Most were buried in mass graves in cemeteries.

The Siege of Leningrad was dramatised for the world. Dimitriy Shostakovitch wrote his Seventh Symphony, the Leningrad Symphony, during the siege. Leningrad came to symbolise the Soviet–Nazi conflict, especially for the Americans. On 9 September 1941, after the start of relentless shelling and air raids, a BBC broadcast said: 'Listen, Leningrad! This is London calling! London is with you. Every shot in Leningrad echoes in London.'

There is a Monument to the Heroic Defenders of Leningrad and a Memorial Museum of Leningrad Defence and the Siege, where you can see original documents and items of that time.

Detail from the Monument to the Heroic Defenders of Leningrad

The Last of the Romanovs

The unhappy reign of the last of the Romanov dynasty, Tsar Nicholas II, started inauspiciously when 3,000 well-wishers were crushed in the crowd at celebrations marking his coronation in 1896. Later, he gained the nickname 'Bloody Nicholas' after peaceful demonstrators were massacred on Palace Square in 1905. But essentially Nicholas was a timid man.

Devoted to his family and his sickly, haemophiliac son Alexis, the Emperor and Autocrat of all the Russias was thought by his cousin Kaiser Wilhelm better cut out to be a 'country gentleman growing turnips'. Despite growing civil unrest and mutinies in the fleet, he preferred to spend most of the year at the royal retreat of Tsarskoe Selo.

Meanwhile, his popularly despised German wife was besotted with the mystic monk Rasputin, whom she believed able to cure her son. Society was scandalised: Rasputin's lewd soirées were common knowledge, yet his power over the royal family seemed total. When Rasputin began to advise on appointments to the Duma during World War I, whilst Nicholas was away at the front, the feeling of unrest increased. Shortly afterwards, Tsar Nicholas' cousin, Grand Duke Dmitri Pavelovich, killed Rasputin, with the help of other family members.

After Rasputin was killed a letter was found forewarning the Romanov family of impending doom:

'I write and leave behind me this letter at St Petersburg. I feel that I shall leave life before January 1 ... If I am killed by common assassins, and especially by my brothers the Russian peasants, you Tsar of Russia, have nothing to fear, remain on your throne of govern, and you, Russian Tsar, will have nothing to fear for your children, they will reign for hundreds of years in Russia. ... if it was your relations who have wrought my death, then no one in the family, that is to say, none of your children or relations, will remain alive for more than two years. They will be killed by the Russian people....You must reflect and act prudently. Think of your safety and tell your relations that I have paid for them with my blood. I shall be killed. I am no longer among the living.'

Finally, the exactions of a deeply unpopular war brought Russia to boiling point. Huge food riots rampaged through Petrograd. The army had revolted. Nicholas signed his abdication in a railway carriage in pencil as 'others do when they make a list of dirty laundry'. On March 2 1917, tsarism died.

Its resting place was to be a mineshaft near Ekaterinburg in the Urals where, in July the following year, Nicholas, his family, servants and the pet spaniel were shot, doused in sulphuric acid and dumped by Bolshevik secret police. The final order to blow up even the building where the murders were committed was given in 1977 by the then local Party chief, Boris Yeltsin.

But it was Yeltsin who promoted the reburial of the rediscovered remains in 1998, in St Petersburg's Cathedral of Sts Peter and Paul – despite the incomprehensible opposition of the Orthodox Church (*see p97*).

Below: The Imperial Throne in Sts Peter and Paul Cathedral

Walk: Nevskiy Prospekt

Nevskiy Prospekt was laid out in the early days of the city and was first known as the Great Perspective Road, running 4.5km (3 miles) from the Admiralty to the Alexander Nevsky Monastery. This main artery reveals a wealth of attractive buildings.

Allow 1 hour.

1 Admiralteystvo (The Admiralty)
A fortified shipyard was built on this site in 1704–11 by the architect A Zakharov. It has been occupied by the Naval Engineering School since 1925.

2 Literaturnoye Kafe (Literary Café)
Once the 'Wolf and Béranger', this café was known for its fashionable clientele. Pushkin left from here for his fatal duel in 1837.

3 Stroganovskiy Dvorets (Stroganovskiy Palace)
Built in 1752–4, in a Baroque style, by the architect B Rastrelli, the building is now used by the Russian Museum for temporary exhibitions. Waxworks of historical figures are on show here.

4 Lyuteranskaya Tserkov (Lutheran Church of St Peter)
The present building was built in 1832–8 by the architect A Briullov.

5 Kazanskiy Sobor (Cathedral of Our Lady of Kazan)
An outstanding example of early 19th-century Russian architecture, it replaced a small stone church and was named after it. Tsar Paul I ordered it to be built after the model of St Peter's in Rome, to hold the ancient icon of Our Lady of Kazan. It is the main Orthodox cathedral of St Petersburg today.

6 Dom Knigi (The House of Books)
It was built for the Singer Sewing Machine Company in 1902–4 by P Syllzor in Art-Nouveau style. This is the biggest bookshop in the city today.
Turn left off Nevskiy Prospekt and head up Naberezhnaya.

7 Khram Spasa na Krovi (Church on the Spilled Blood)
The church stands on the site of the assassination of Tsar Alexander II. It was built in 1887–1907 by the architects A Parland and I Makarov. Over 20 types of minerals including jasper and marble are lavished on the mosaics of the iconostasis, icon cases, canopy and floor.
Return along Naberezhnaya and turn left to continue along Nevskiy Prospekt.

8 Maliy Zal Filarmonii (Small Hall of the State Academic Philharmonic)
This was the main concert hall of the city from 1826 to 1846. Here, outstanding musicians including Liszt, Schumann and Rubinstein performed.

9 Tserkov Svyatoy Ekaterini (Roman Catholic Church of St Catherine)

Built in 1762–83 by J B Vallin de la Mothe, the church is a fine example of the transitional period between Baroque and neo-classical styles.

10 Gostiniy Dvor

Strictly neo-classical in outline, this bazaar was completed in 1785. The shopping centre has more than 300 outlets, which sell everything from cosmetics to souvenirs.

11 Rossiyskaya Natsionalnaya Biblioteka (Russian National Library)

The library was opened in1814 and is the fifth-largest library in the world. *Turn right off Nevskiy Prospekt and cross Aleksandriyskaya Ploshchad to reach the Aleksandriyskiy Teatro.*

12 Aleksandriyskiy Teatr (Aleksandriyskiy Theatre)

Once named after A Pushkin, the theatre was built in 1828–32 by C Rossi. *Retrace your steps and turn right on Nevskiy Prospekt.*

13 Anichkov Dvorets (Anichkov Palace)

Built in 1816–18, the palace was a gift from Tsarina Elizabeth to her lover Aleksey Razumovskiy. Today it houses the Palace of Youth Creativity.

14 Anichkov Most (Anichkov Bridge)

It is famous for its four bronze statues of men taming horses by P Klodt.

15 Beloselskiy-Belozerskiy Dvorets (Beloselskiy–Belozerskiy Palace)

Designed by A Stakenschneider in 1847–8, it is now a cultural centre.

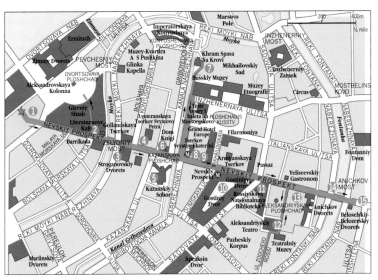

Walk: Neva West Bank to the Griboyedov Canal

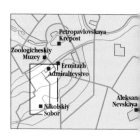

The splendours of the Admiralty, the imperial metropolis, the unnerving haunt of historical spectres … the district west of Palace Square captures the essence of St Petersburg. *Allow 2 hours.*

Start at the Admiralty at the end of Nevskiy Prospekt.

Turn away from the river and make for St Isaac's Cathedral.

1 Admiralteystvo (The Admiralty)

A fortified shipyard was built on this site in 1704–11. In 1806, A Zhakharov started to rebuild the Admiralty, which has been home of the Naval Engineering School since 1925. *Walk through the Admiralty garden to Decembrists' Square.*

2 Ploshchad Dekabristov (Decembrists' Square)

This square was named after the uprising of Guards Officers on 14 December 1825, when troops gathered at the far end of the square to demand constitutional reform. Nicholas I easily crushed the rebellion. The poet Pushkin escaped with a warning, surviving to pen his epic *The Bronze Horseman*, its title taken from the statue of Peter the Great in the square (Medniy Vsadnik). A French sculptor, E Falconet, spent over 12 years on this project.

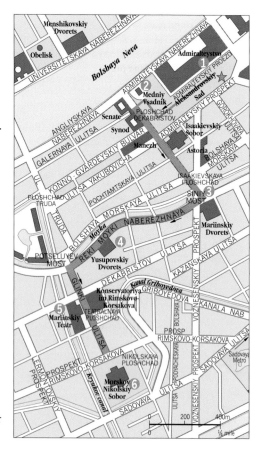

3 Isaakievskaya Ploshchad (St Isaac's Square)

St Isaac's Cathedral, designed in 1818 by A de Montferrand, gives its name to the impressive square beyond, created in the reign of Nicholas I. Across the 100m (328ft)-wide Blue Bridge, broadest in the city, *Mariinskiy Dvorets* (Mariinskiy Palace) dominates the southern end of the square. Now the City Legislative Chamber, it was built in 1844 for the daughter of Nicholas I, whose equestrian statue stands in the centre of the square. On the east is the Astoria Hotel, designed by F Lidval in Art-Nouveau style in 1910–12.
Cross the Moyka River and follow the embankment westwards.

4 Yusupovskiy Dvorets (Yusupov Palace)

This was the residence of the fabulously rich Prince Felix Yusupov and scene of the 1916 assassination of Rasputin who was enticed to the basement, poisoned and shot in the head, but refused to die even when beaten and shot another four times. The terrified conspirators then threw him in the river where he drowned.
Continue along the embankment and turn left on to Glinki Ulitsa to Theatre Square.

5 Teatralnaya Ploshchad (Theatre Square)

Once the site for fairs and festivals, here the Mariinskiy Theatre and Rimsky-Korsakov Conservatory were established in the 19th century. The ballet dancers Anna Pavlova and Vaslav Nijinsky created a sensation at the theatre, while the conservatory nurtured the composers Dmitriy Shostakovich and Igor Stravinsky.
Continue along Glinki Ulitsa to St Nicholas Naval Cathedral.

6 Morskoy Nikolskiy Sobor (St Nicholas' Naval Cathedral)

Standing at the junction of the Kryukov and Griboyedov canals, this was built in 1753–62 in a Baroque style, by the architect Savva Chevakinskiy, for sailors and Admiralty employees. Saint Nicholas is the patron saint of sailors.
Walk back to Nevskiy Prospekt, either along the north or south bank of the Griboyedov Canal or directly along Sadovaya Ulitsa.

The monument to the founder of St Petersburg, Peter the Great

Walk: The Winter Palace to the Summer Garden

This short stroll encompasses the sites of two regicides, the home of Russia's greatest poet, two royal palaces and the Summer Garden.

Allow 2 hours.

Start on the eastern side of Dvortsovaya Ploshchad (Palace Square, see pp100–1).

1 The River Moyka

Crossing Pevcheskiy Most (Singers' Bridge) to the right bank of the winding Moyka, you are faced with the Glinka Kapella, St Petersburg's oldest concert hall and once headquarters of the celebrated Imperial Court Choir.

A little further on, at Reki Moyki Naberezhnaya 12, Russia's national poet Alexander Pushkin lived in the first-floor apartments (*see pp112–13*). The poet's funeral took place in the Equerries' Church which occupies the central block of the Imperial Stables, commanding Konyushennaya Ploshchad to the right from the river.

Continue across the square to the bridge over the Griboyedov Canal.

The Admiralty

2 Khram Spasa na Krovi (Church on the Spilled Blood)

St Petersburg's most incongruous church is a near copy of St Basil's Cathedral in Moscow, its Orthodox design reflecting the surge in nationalist feeling at the time. It commemorates the assassination of Alexander II; the altar stands over the place where the tsar was blown up by a revolutionary bomb in 1881 – hence 'on the spilled blood'.
Head north, once more crossing the Moyka.

3 Marsovo Pole (The Field of Mars)

The open expanse north of the Moyka became an imperial parade ground. The eternal flame in the centre honours the 180 dead of the 1917 February Revolution buried here, and the fallen of the October Revolution and Civil War.

The Mramorniy Dvorets (Marble Palace) of 1785 at the far end of the square was built for Catherine the Great's lover, Count Grigori Orlov, who managed to lose it twice gambling at cards.
Enter the Summer Garden through the beautiful wrought-iron grille from the embankment.

4 Letniy Sad and Letniy Dvorets (Summer Garden and Summer Palace)

The recently refurbished Summer Garden was laid out informally after a flood in 1777 washed away Peter the Great's more ambitious pastiche of the gardens of Versailles.

Peter's Summer Palace (1710) is characteristically modest. His wife lived on the first floor while Peter busied himself in the turnery or at raucous banquets below. The park is more tranquil than in Peter's day, when he would order the nobility to join in his compulsory 'drinking assemblies'.
Letniy Sad Open: 10am–9.30pm (to dusk in winter). Admission charge in summer.
Letniy Dvorets tel: 314 0456. Open: 11am–5pm May–Oct. Closed: Tue and the last Fri of the month.
Leaving the Summer Garden, take the Fontanka left bank to the Engineer's Castle.

5 Inzhenerniy Zamok (Engineer's Castle)

The curious architecture of the Engineer's Castle (1801) was once surrounded by a moat to protect Paul I, terrified of assassination. He hurried the construction of his redoubt, plundering the site of the unfinished St Isaac's Cathedral. But Paul died mere days after he had moved in, throttled in his nightshirt by courtiers and army officers exasperated by their tsar's accelerating insanity. The building takes its name from the Engineering Academy to which it was transferred. Today this building belongs to the Russian Museum for temporary exhibitions.
A short walk south brings you to Nevskiy Prospekt or Ploshchad Iskusstv and the Russian Museum (see pp106–7).

Walk: Basil Island and the Spit

The majestic view of the Neva delta from the spit of Basil (Vasilevskiy) Island readily conjures up the dream of maritime grandeur that obsessed Peter the Great. Embracing some of the city's oldest buildings, the island's streets still evoke the breathtaking imperial self-confidence that fired the tsar's vision.

Allow 2 hours, excluding museum visits.

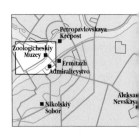

Start at Vasileostrovskaya metro station. Turn right down 6 and 7 Lines (linii).

1 To Bolshoy Prospekt

Make for the pink bell tower of the Andreevskiy Sobor (Cathedral of St Andrew) of 1780, with a wonderful iconostasis in its lofty vaulted interior.

Turning left along leafy Bolshoy Prospekt, note No 6 where Tatyana Savicheva, whose diary is exhibited at the Piskaryovskoe Cemetery, recorded the starvation of her family during the siege. The 1771 Luteranskaya Tserkov Svaytoy Yekateriny (Lutheran Church of St Catherine) stands opposite.

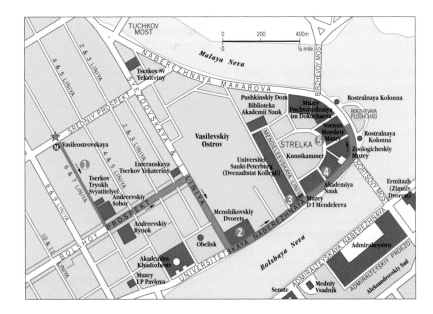

Turn right on to 1 Line (liniya), passing to the left the former Imperial Cadet barracks, site of Lenin's first bid for power at the Soviet of Workers' and Soldiers' Deputies in June 1917. At the river turn left on to Universitetskaya Naberezhnaya.

2 Menshikovskiy Dvorets (Menshikov Palace)

Ochre paintwork and Dutch-style gables characterise the palace built from 1710 to 1720 for Peter's friend and favourite Alexander Menshikov (1673–1729), first governor of the city.

The rooms inside have been carefully restored, the highlights being the tiled first-floor quarters, the lathe at which Peter amused himself, and the kitchen's enormous wooden beer vessel – big enough for the duo's fabled bawdy dinner parties.

Menshikov's luck turned after the deaths of Peter and his wife (Menshikov's former mistress) Catherine I, and he died in Siberian exile, penniless.

The palace is now a branch of the Hermitage, with an exhibition on Russian culture from 1700 to the 1730s. *Tel: 323 1112. www.ermitazhmuseum.org. Tours: 10.30am–4.30pm. Closed: Mon. Admission charge.*

3 Zdaniye Dvenadtsati Kollegiy (The Twelve Colleges Building)

Among St Petersburg's oldest buildings, the Colleges were built for Peter's bureaucracy. Given to the University in 1819, they became an epicentre of militancy. Lenin graduated from the law faculty, but soon abandoned law to devote himself to revolution.

The Spit of Basil Island

A statue of the great polymath Mikhail Lomonosov (1708–65) divides the Colleges from the Neo-Classical Akademiya Nauk (Academy of Sciences). *Continue along the embankment.*

4 Muzey Antropologii i Etnografii (Museum of Anthropology and Ethnography)

This museum is also known as the Kunstkammer. Peter's fascination with science led him during a trip to Holland to purchase the collection of anatomical oddities at the heart of Russia's first museum (1718). Free vodka enticed visitors to gaze at pickled bottled freaks that, over 250 years on, have lost none of their power to shock. (*See p110.*) *Return to the embankment passing the Zoological Museum (see p111).*

5 The Spit (Strelka)

Commanding a superb view of the SS Peter and Paul Fortress and the Winter Palace, the Strelka – or island spit – is a St Petersburg symbol.

The Stock Exchange, now the Voenno Morskoy Muzey (Naval Museum – *see p111*), dominates the Strelka, flanked by former warehouses and the defunct Customs House, mute witnesses to the commercial hubbub once focused here.

Walk: The Smolniy District

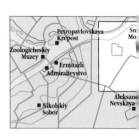

Intimately connected with the events of 1917, this peaceful residential district conceals its violent history behind the tranquil Tauride Gardens and the stunning cathedral of the Smolniy Convent.

Allow 2 hours.

Start at metro Chernyshevskaya and turn right out of the metro and right again down Furshtadskaya Ulitsa.

1 Tavricheskiy Sad (Tauride Gardens)

Quiet Furshtadskaya Ulitsa leads to the gates of the Tauride Gardens, where statues of Tchaikovsky and the poet Esenin preside over squealing children, strolling pensioners and inebriated fishermen in one of St Petersburg's most attractive parks.

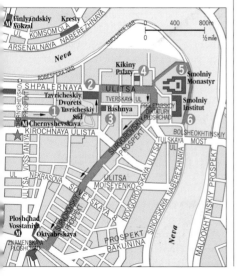

2 Tavricheskiy Dvorets (Tauride Palace)

In the far left corner of the park stands the celebrated Tauride Palace, site of the first 'Duma' or parliament in 1906. After the Revolution, Lenin sent Red Guards in to disband the first and last sitting of the elected Constituent Assembly in 1918.

Built in 1789, the palace was a gift from Catherine the Great to her lover Prince Grigori Potemkin as a reward for the conquest of Tauris, the old name of the Crimea. In one of his frequent fits of hatred for his mother, her son Paul donated the palace to the Horse Guards for stables. (Closed to the public.)

Leave the park and go down Tavricheskaya Ulitsa towards Shpalernaya Ulitsa.

3 Bashnya ('The Tower')

Building No 35 on the corner of Tverskaya Ulitsa is famed for its top-floor apartment, dubbed 'The Tower'. It was the meeting place of one of Russia's greatest avant-garde circles, including the poets Anna Akhmatova, Alexander Blok, Osip Mandelstam and Nikolai Gumilyov. Predictably, most of them were exiled, executed or silenced by the Bolsheviks.

Head right down Shpalernaya Ulitsa.

4 Kikiny Palaty (Kikin's Chambers)

The view of the Smolniy Cathedral is breathtaking as you approach the convent along Shpalernaya Ulitsa, but it is worth looking at the beautifully preserved building on the left near the junction with Stavropolskaya Ulitsa. It briefly belonged to one of Peter the Great's senior bureaucrats, Alexander Kikin, before he suffered public torture and execution on Moscow's Red Square for befriending Peter's estranged son, Alexis.

5 Smolniy Monastyr (Smolniy Convent)

One of St Petersburg's highlights, the icy grandeur of the Smolniy Convent is the work of the great architect Bartolomeo Rastrelli. The design, commissioned by Empress Elizabeth in 1748, originally included a vertiginous 140m (459ft) bell tower, now reduced to 63m (207ft).

The convent's brief religious life – in 1797 it became a home for widows of the nobility – may explain the unimaginative cathedral interior. A vegetable depot during the Civil War, it now serves as an exhibition centre. You can climb up the bell tower to enjoy the view over the Neva.

(The name 'Smolniy' (*smola* – tar) is derived from the shipbuilders' tar yards on the site in Peter's time.)
Tel: 271 9182. Open: 11am–4pm. Closed: Thur. Admission charge.

6 Smolniy Institut (The Smolniy Institute)

Adjoining the convent, the former Smolniy Institute was Russia's first school for girls, but is better known as the nerve centre from which Trotsky and Lenin plotted the Bolshevik Revolution. As the Leningrad Party headquarters it also witnessed the murder of Party boss Sergei Kirov in 1934, marking the inception of Stalin's savage purges.

Closed to the public, the building is now the Governor's office. *Return along Survorovskiy Prospekt by trolleybus 5, 7, 11 or 16 to Ploshchad Vosstaniya metro.*

Smolniy Convent, designed by Bartolomeo Rastrelli

Excursions from St Petersburg

St Petersburg is surrounded by a necklace of world-famous suburbs, most former residences of the emperors. It is impossible to come to St Petersburg and not admire the palaces and parks which are jewels of architecture.

The gilded domes of Catherine Palace

GATCHINA
In 1765 Catherine the Great presented this village to her lover, Prince Orlov, who commissioned A Rinaldi to build a Neo-Classical palace, which was completed in 1781.
Leningrad region, Gatchina, Krasnoarmeyskiy Prospekt 1. Tel: 712 1509. www.alexanderpalace.org/gatchina. Open: 10am–6pm. Closed: Mon and the first Tue of the month.
How to get there: suburban train from the Baltiysky terminus, or coach.

KRONSTADT
This sea-fortress and port has over 300 historic structures, including fortifications and the Sea Cathedral.
How to get there: bus 510/510-E from Staraya Derevnya metro station to Kronstadt; or train from Baltiysky terminus to Oranienbaum, bus 6 to Oranienbaum quay and then ferry to Kronstadt. In summer, the hydrofoil-vessel Meteor *runs from the quay near Tuchkov Bridge to Kronstadt quay.*

LAKE LADOGA
Kizhi
This peaceful island serves as an outdoor museum of 18th-century wooden architecture. The Cathedral of the Transfiguration has 22 unpainted wooden domes.
How to get there: boat over Lake Ladoga to Valaam and Kizhi; operates end of May to end of Sept.

Valaam
In the northern part of Lake Ladoga lie Valaam Island and about 50 smaller ones. Valaam is one of Russia's most ancient and important monasteries, known as the Northern Athos. *Further details: www.valaam.ru*

NOVGOROD THE GREAT
Founded in 862, Novgorod is Russia's oldest town. At its heart is the Cathedral of St Sophia built in 1045. Since Novgorod was the place where the first prince of Russia ruled, a monument to commemorate 1000 years of Russia was built near to the cathedral by M Mikeshin in 1862.
Tourist Office, tel: (8162) 773074. http://eng.tourism.velikynovgorod.ru. How to get there: suburban train from the Moskovskiy terminal, or by coach.

ORANIENBAUM (LOMONOSOV)
Prince Menshikov began a palace and park in the early 18th century. The future Peter III lived here 1743–61 and

commissioned A Rinaldi to build him a modest palace. The most unusual building is Rinaldi's Sliding Pavilion.
48 Dvortsovy Prospekt, 189510 Lomonosov. Tel: 422 4796, 423 1641. Open: 10am–5pm, Mon 11am–5pm. Closed: Tue. Admission charge.
How to get there: suburban train from the Baltiysky terminus, or coach.

PAVLOVSK

Catherine the Great presented this palace to her son, Grand Duke Paul, in 1777. Its architects, the greatest of the period, were C Cameron, V Brenna, G Quarenghi, A Voronikhin and C Rossi.
20 Revolutsii St, Pavlovsk. Tel: 470 6155/ 6536. www.pavlovsk.org. Open: 10am–5pm. Closed: Fri. Admission charge.

PETERHOF (PETRODVORETS)

In 1704 Peter I built a wooden house here so he could oversee the construction of the island fortress of Kronstadt. The palace, built in 1713–23, was extended by Tsarina Elizabeth.

Bolshoi Dvorets (Grand Palace)

Filled with lavish rooms and galleries, this dominates the estate. The 144 fountains on the estate are linked by a water main with springs welling out in the Ropshinsky Heights. The Upper Park has as its centrepiece the Neptune Fountain. The Lower Park has the famous Great Cascade.
2 Razvodnaya St. Tel: 427 7425. www.peterhof.org. Open: 10.30am–6pm. Closed: Mon; last Tue of month. Admission charge.
How to get there: suburban train from the Baltiysky terminus, or coach.

TSARSKOYE SELO (PUSHKIN)

Peter the Great regained this place, 24km (15 miles) south of St Petersburg, from Sweden. It was then a farmstead. Peter gave it to Prince Menshikov, but later took it back to give to his wife, the future Catherine I. It was the first town with electricity in Europe.
www.tsar.ru.
How to get there: suburban train from the Vitebsky terminus, or coach.

Aleksandrovskiy Dvorets (Alexander Palace)

Built in the late 18th century by the architect G Quarenghi for Alexander I. You can also admire the Alexander Park.
2 Dvortsovaya St, Tsarskoye Selo. Tel: 466 6071. Open: 10am–5pm. Closed: Tue; last Wed of month. Admission charge.

Catherine Palace

Tsarskoye Selo's oldest building, this was rebuilt in 1752 by Rastrelli for Tsarina Elizabeth, who named it after her mother, Catherine I. One of the most beautiful rooms is the Amber Room, a gift from Frederick William I of Prussia.
7 Sadovaya St, Tsarskoye Selo. Tel: 465 5308. Open: 10am–5pm. Closed: Tue; last Mon of month. Admission charge.

Litsey (Lyceum)

Pushkin's presence can be felt in Tsarskoye Selo Park, to which he dedicated verses, and in the Lyceum, where he went to school.
2 Sadovaya St, Tsarskoye Selo. Tel: 476 6411. Open: 10.30am–5pm. Closed: Tue; last Mon of month. Admission charge.

Getting Away From It All

Even the most hardened sightseer is likely to tire of the hectic pace, frantic crowds and traffic fumes of Moscow and St Petersburg. Fortunately, both cities offer a variety of means of escape; they may sometimes involve a little travelling, but the results are worth it. The following entries are just a few of the many excursions on offer.

A sea of tulips and the Rostral Column in Strelka

MOSCOW
Arkhangelskoye
Prince Golitsyn's magnificent country house is the highlight of this beautiful spot just outside the city. The house was built of stucco-covered timber by Rastrelli, architect of St Petersburg's Winter Palace, and is luxuriously appointed with tapestries and 18th-century furniture. The estate's landscaped gardens lead down to the Moskva River in a series of terraces.
Krasnogorsk Region. Tel: 363 1375. www.arkhangelskoe.ru. Open: Wed–Sun 10am–5pm. Admission charge. Metro: Tushinskaya, then bus 549 to Arkhangelskoye stop.

Bukhta Radostyei (Bay of Joys)
Half an hour's hydrofoil (*raketa*) ride from the river boat terminal at Rechnoy Vokzal metro brings you to the 'Bay of Joys', a popular riverside picnic spot in the warmer months. Stock up with a loaf of black bread, sausage, pickled herrings, cheese and a bottle of Georgian red wine.
Phone the Moscow River Boat Company for departure and last return times.

Leningradskoye Shosse 59. Tel: 459 7270/ 7091. www.rechflot.ru (Russian only). Metro: Rechnoy Vokzal.

Boulevards and parks
You need not travel far to escape Moscow's urban intensity – a stroll along the ring of boulevards in the town centre is often enough to restore a little sanity. Tverskoy, Gogolevskiy and Rozhdestvenskiy Boulevards are among the best for people-watching, as old men argue over chessboards in summer and fur-coated toddlers are taken for gentle sledge rides in winter.

Alternatively, head for the forested parks on the outskirts of town. Izmaylovskiy Park and Bittsa Forest are two of the best.
Metro: Izmaylovskiy Park, Bittsevskiy Park.

Kolomenskoye
Peter the Great spent much of his childhood at this ancient and picturesque estate on the Moskva River. Originally a 14th-century village of artisans and fishermen, its commanding location made it a strategic point in

Muscovy's seemingly ceaseless battles. Dmitri Donskoy massed his troops on the hill before the decisive battle of Kulikovo in 1380. Ivan the Terrible made it the first stage of his campaign to capture the Tartar stronghold of Kazan. Many of the wizened oak trees still standing were even then already several centuries old.

Today the site is an open-air museum, Muzey-Zapovednik XVI–XVII vi 'Kolomenskoye'. The rugged beauty of the 1532 Church of the Ascension is the chief attraction, closely followed by the azure cupolas of the Church of Our Lady of Kazan visible through the estate gateway. A number of unique wooden buildings were transferred to the estate in the 1930s, including the simple log cabin from which Peter directed his northern campaigns, a defence tower from the White Sea and a 17th-century mead distillery from the nearby village of Preobrazhenskoye.

A great place for sledging and cross-country skiing in winter, Kolomenskoye is at its most enchanting as the sun sets and a largely elderly congregation gathers for evening prayers at the Kazan Church.
Prospekt Andropova 39. Tel: 115 2309. Grounds open year round. Buildings open: 10am–6pm. Closed: Mon. Admission charge for the small decorative arts museum. Metro: Kolomenskaya, then follow the signs to the estate.

Kuntsevo

The woodlands on the steep river banks between Kuntsevskaya and Bagrationovskaya metro stations are ideal for a summer picnic or for tobogganing in winter. On a clear day in autumn, the view across the river through the orange and crimson sycamore trees is stunning.
Metro: Kuntsevskaya. Exit on to Malaya Filyovskaya Ulitsa, walk 300m (984ft)

A tree-lined pathway invites a quiet stroll

St Petersburg's Catherine Canal. The pace is slow and the scenes evocative

back towards the centre and cut up through the apartment blocks to the woodlands beyond.

Kuskovo

On the outskirts of Moscow, the Kuskovo estate is a wonderful escape from the city. It was built in the 18th century for Count Sheremetev (*see p60*), owner of over a million hectares (4,000sq miles) of land. Although ravaged by Napoleon's troops in 1812, a fine ensemble of Russian architecture remains, surrounded by a landscaped park and lake.

The two-storey wooden palace, once the scene of Sheremetev's lavish society balls, retains its opulent interior decoration and forms part of a museum of ceramics on the estate, made up of private collections nationalised after the Revolution.

The estate is also the setting for a summer season of evening concerts – check listings in the press.
Ulitsa Yunosti 2. Tel: 370 0160. Open: (summer) Wed–Sun 10am–6pm, (winter) Wed–Sun 10am–4pm. Closed: last Wed of month. Admission charge. Metro: Ryazanskiy Prospekt, Vikhino.

Serebryany Bor ('Silver Pine Forest')

This secluded island on the Moskva River is a favourite destination of Muscovites on hot summer weekends. Communist Party officials built the many exclusive dachas here, now being bought up by the capital's new ruling class of businessmen because of the relatively clean location upstream of heavy industry. For those not tempted to swim, the island is a great place to indulge the Russian passion for hunting mushrooms and berries.

Take trolleybus 21 from Polezhayevskaya metro along Prospekt Marshala Zhukova right on to the island.

A boat cruise will offer you a different perspective from which to view the city

Tsaritsyno

Surrounded by forested parks and ornamental lakes, the picturesque ruins at Tsaritsyno in the south of the city are all that remain of one of Moscow's strangest royal retreats. It was designed in red brick and limestone by Vasili Bazhenov, in a peculiar cocktail of architectural styles, for Catherine the Great. Visiting Moscow in 1787, Catherine was appalled by Tsaritsyno, reportedly describing the turret pavilions as akin to candles around a coffin. With wars against the Turks consuming ever more of the imperial budget, Tsaritsyno was never completed. The park's ornamental bridges and several of the estate's buildings, including Bazhenov's Opera House, have been undergoing restoration. Boats can be hired on the lakes in summer.

Access to Tsaritsyno and the parks is free. Metro: Tsaritsyno. Leave the station from the exit nearer the front of the train, head under the railway bridges, take the right fork, turning left at the lakes to the estate entrance.

Fun and games on Serebryany Bor

Russian Winter

A time of picturesque charm and long, cold nights; of festivities; of perilous streets and treacherous pavements ... winter is the quintessential Russian experience.

The first frosts set in at the end of *babye lyeto* – 'woman's summer' – a brief spell of warmer weather in autumn compared to the last flowering of female beauty before old age. Apart from occasional short-lived thaws, the winter in Moscow and St Petersburg lasts through to early March and the festival of Maslenitsa, its pagan origins alive in the roaring bonfires and orgiastic consumption of the soured-cream-doused pancakes – *blini* – that symbolise the sun.

On 31 December Russian children sleep restlessly in anticipation of what Ded-Moroz – 'Grandfather Frost' – and his girl helper Snegurochka will bring for Novy God – New Year – still the biggest Russian holiday.

On a more mundane level, the all-encompassing *slyakot* – a singularly Russian mixture of mud, slush and sleet that accompanies the thaw – means going out armed with a change of shoes. Everybody wears furs, but note: hell hath no fury like a cloakroom attendant who discovers your coat is missing the loop for hanging. Similarly, *babushkas* verbally lambast mothers on the street whose children they consider inadequately dressed.

Since 988, when Prince Vladimir of Kiev rejected Islam in favour of Christianity (because the former's condemnation of alcohol was unsuitable to the Russian climate), the colder months have been the occasion for increased drinking, and each winter brings its toll of deaths by frostbite of the homeless and those who were reckless enough to stop for a snooze on the way home from a boisterous night out.

Snow and ice bring out tobogganing children, couples skating the iced paths of Gorky Park, and an army of the tracksuited elderly cruising the woods on cross-country skis. Strangest of all are the ice swimmers, nicknamed

morzh ('walruses'), whose ideal pastime in a heavy frost is to strip down and plunge into gaps in the ice before setting off on a barefooted jog across the snow.

Russian people are used to winter and Moscow's location makes even very low temperatures more bearable than anywhere else. Even so, be prepared that during occasional severe conditions you might be stuck indoors for a couple of days. You might be forced to take short walks, hopping from sight to sight, or follow the Russian example of hopping from one vodka stall to another.

Opposite: Even winter Moscow has its magic
Above top: Snow is a source of enjoyment for children …
Above: … while their mothers have time to show off their new fur hats or coats

ST PETERSBURG
Finskiy Zaliv (Gulf of Finland)

Three capital cities – St Petersburg, Tallinn and Helsinki – stand on the Gulf of Finland. If you have time for a paddle in summer or a walk on the ice in winter, its north shore has sandy beaches and shaded woodland where many citizens have their summer dachas. Slightly inland, Lake Razliv is a favourite picnic spot near the town of Sestroretsk 34km (21 miles). Further up the coast is the village of Repino 50km (30 miles), named after the painter Ilya Repin, whose estate is now a museum.

Griffin guarding Bank Bridge

Museum of I Repin

Visitors can see the artist's study, dining room and studio. The grounds and setting are extremely picturesque.
Primorskoye Shosse 411. Open: 10am–5pm. Closed: Tue. Admission charge. How to get there: suburban train from the Finland terminus (for the coast, pick one going to Sestroretsk and get off at any attractive spot; for Repino, any train headed for Zelenogorsk); or taxi-bus along Primorskoye Shosse, the coast road.

Griboyedov Canal

Without leaving the city centre, a stroll along the banks of the former Catherine Canal is a good way to unwind. Starting at Nevskiy Prospekt, pass the Cathedral of Our Lady of Kazan, and walk up to Kryukov Canal towards New Holland (Novaya Gollandiya) island with its melancholy atmosphere. This island, once used for storing ship timber, was

Interior room at Elagin Palace

The Gulf of Finland

named after the Dutch shipbuilders who inspired Peter the Great. You can join boat tours from Nevskiy Prospekt, on the Griboyedov Canal, Fontanka River or Moyka River.

Kirov Islands

If you wish to escape the city, Elagin Island is for you. The palace grounds, now the Central Park of Culture and Rest (famous for its water attractions), make up most of the island. Its centrepiece is the Elagin Palace, built in 1822 for the mother of Tsar Alexander I. In summer, you can hire boats here or take a cruise on the gulf of Finland. Kamenniy (Stone) is the island of recreation and relaxation, boasting many historic aristocratic mansions and also an 18th-century palace, built by Catherine the Great for her son, Paul.

Krestovskiy Island is best known for its sports stadium, but is also an attractive area for walking.

Urn on the steps at Elagin Palace

S h o p p i n g

Nowadays, shopping, in Moscow and St Petersburg at least, is no longer the nightmarish experience it once was. On the contrary, if you have the money you can buy just about anything you might need on your trip or as a souvenir – everything from lacquerware and ceramics to vodka and CDs. When shopping in the souvenir markets, especially, be sure to compare prices as there are plenty of hustlers and conmen about. That way you'll get what you are paying for.

Traditional Russian 3-string balalaika

Shopping in Russia

When embarking on a shopping spree, you should remember that there are broadly two kinds of store in Russia.

The Western-managed shops function just as you would expect and may accept credit cards. Sales assistants often speak English. Even if they do not, they will be attentive and helpful.

In the former state stores expect to queue to see the goods, queue to pay for them and then queue to hand over the receipt and receive your purchase. Although shelves are better stocked than formerly, sales assistants are still extraordinarily rude, despite a decree by the Moscow mayor that shopkeepers are obliged to be nice to customers! Do not stand on ceremony – if you wait to be noticed, you will not leave the shop before nightfall. Lastly, do not forget to bring your own bag since few Russian shops provide them.

Russian gourmet stores offer delicacies that will suit everyone

Souvenirs

Amber, gold, furs, lacquerware, glossy art books, CDs, caviar, vodka and domestic brandies and 'champagne' are all good value in Russia. (Remember customs regulations, however – *see p180.*)

The market in Soviet memorabilia is stronger than ever. Ironic 'Leninist' T-shirts, Soviet-era bric-a-brac and odd items of military apparel – you'll find them all in the tourist fleamarkets. Bear in mind, though, that old uniforms and army belts are unlikely to be originals. More traditional favourites are gaudily painted mugs, plates and spoons from the village of Khokhloma outside Moscow, 'Matryoshka' stacking dolls and elaborately lacquered boxes (*palekh*). Fake versions of all these will be earnestly offered to you at the markets; to be safe, it is advisable to confine serious purchases to specialist souvenir shops where the more you pay the better your chances of obtaining the real thing.

The Moscow haven for souvenir hunters is the Izmaylovskiy Market, open at weekends and selling everything from fighter pilots' helmets and stolen icons to handmade jewellery and traditional costumes. Bargain hard (but see **Customs**, *p180*). Turn left out of metro Izmaylovskiy Park and pass the high-rise hotel complex. The market gates are in front of you.

The equivalent in St Petersburg is Klenovaya Alleya, open daily in the season. From metro Gostiniy Dvor, head towards Ploshchad Iskusstv and turn right along Inzhenernaya Ulitsa.

Both cities also have open-air art bazaars selling local contemporary work. The main centre in Moscow is opposite the entrance to Gorky Park (*metro Park Kultury*), in St Petersburg along Nevskiy Prospekt.

Moscow's souvenir shops include **Yantar** (*All Russia Exhibition Centre, no. 66 (Cultural Pavilion). Metro: VDNKh*), which specialises in amber jewellery, chessboards, mosaics etc. **Dom Farfora** (*Leninskiy Prospekt 36. Tel: 137 6023. Closed Sun. Metro: Leninskiy Prospekt, then walk*) has an enormous range of porcelain, crystal and glass. **The Arbat** is also worth a browse.

In St Petersburg, try **Lomonosov porcelain** (*Nevskiy Prospekt 160. Tel: 277 4838. Metro: Ploshchad Aleksandr Nevskovo*). This outlet of one of Europe's oldest porcelain factories is better value than the better-known shop in the Grand Hotel Europe. **Passazh** (*Nevskiy Prospekt 48. Metro: Nevskiy Prospekt/Gostiniy Dvor*): several shops in this beautiful late 19th-century shopping centre sell good-quality

Famous Russian lacquered boxes are sold almost everywhere

porcelain, glassware and antiques as well as other souvenirs.

Books

Useful bookshops in Moscow include **Biblio-Globus** (*Ulitsa Myasnitskaya 6. Tel: 928 3567. www.biblio-globus.ru. Metro: Lubyanka*), **Don innostranoy knigi** (*Ulitsa Kuznetskiy most 18. Tel: 928 2021. Metro: Kuznetskiy most*) and **Shakespeare & co.** (*1-y Novokuznetsiy pereulok 5/7. Tel: 951 9360. Closed Sun. Metro: Novokuznetskaya/ Paveletskaya*).

Bookworms in St Petersburg can visit **Dom Knigi** (House of Books), the largest book store in the city with books in numerous languages.
28 and 62 Nevskiy Prospekt. Tel: 318 6546. Metro: Nevskiy Prospekt/Gostiniy Dvor.

CAVIAR AND 'COGNAC'

Caviar is easily available in any large food shop. It may be cheaper on the streets, but it may not be caviar – it is not unheard of for tourists to buy ball bearings in axle grease from especially enterprising salesmen.

Locally produced drinks have all but disappeared from the streets under the deluge of imported beverages, but are nevertheless worth seeking out. Armenian '*konyak*' (brandy) is highly thought of outside the former USSR, as are Georgian and Crimean wines. Another fine souvenir is real Russian Smirnovskaya vodka, recognisable by its tapering bottle. Try the following outlets:

Moscow:

Novoarbatskiy Gastronom

Ulitsa Novy Arbat 13. Tel: 291 5828. Metro: Arbatskaya/Smolenskaya.

St Petersburg:

Yeliseyev's

Nevskiy Prospekt 56. Metro: Gostiniy Dvor. This historic store with a stunning Style Moderne interior has an excellent selection of caviar, vodka, cognac and smoked fish.

There is plenty of caviar on offer, but make sure it is the genuine article

DEPARTMENT STORES

Moscow:

Gosudarstvenny Universalniy Magazin (GUM)

Moscow's chief department store translates in typical Soviet style as State Department Store, and is better known as GUM (pronounced 'goom'). The impressive building's vast glass canopy covers galleried shops within, once packed only with shoddy electrical devices, outsize bras and queues. Now privatised, it is a mall to rival Paris's best. Europe's classiest boutiques are rapidly edging out the old state shops.

Krasnaya Ploshchad 3. Tel: 921 5763. www.gum.ru. Metro: Ploshchad Revolyutsii.

Petrovskiy Passazh

Petrovka Ulitsa 10. Metro: Teatralnaya.

TsUM

Petrovka Ulitsa 2. Tel: 292 1157/7600. www.tsum.ru. Metro: Teatralnaya.

St Petersburg:

Gostiniy Dvor complex

Nevskiy Prospekt 35. www.lgd.ru. Metro: Gostiniy Dvor.

Passazh

Nevskiy Prospekt 48. Metro: Nevskiy Prospekt/Gostiniy Dvor.

FURS

A lot of furs on sale are Scandinavian, so ask if you want the Russian article.

Moscow:

Furs

Pyatniskaya 13. Tel: 951 9880. Metro: Novokuznetskaya/Tretyakovskaya.

Sovmekhastoria

Ulitsa Bolshaya Dorogomilovskaya 14. Tel: 323 4384. Metro: Kievskaya. Also at *Petrovka 17. Tel: 928 1548.*

Metro: Kuznetskiy most.
Several shops in the GUM arcade on
Red Square also sell furs.

St Petersburg:
Lena
Nevskiy Prospekt 50. Tel: 918 4056.
www.lenafur.ru. Metro: Nevskiy Prospekt.

SPORTS SUPPLIES
Moscow:
Sportmaster
Bolshaya Sadovaya 1. www.sportmaster.ru.
Metro: Mayakovskaya.
Skates, skis, rucksacks, clothing, trainers,
etc. are available from this chain.

St Petersburg:
Sportmaster
Moskovskiy Prospekt 10–12. Tel: 320 0003.
www.sportmaster.ru. Metro: Sadovaya.

SUPERMARKETS
Both cities are dotted with foreign-run
supermarkets which sell a wide range of
food, toiletries and the like. Prices are
higher than in most European countries.

Moscow:
Armeniya
Tverskaya 17. Metro: Tverskaya.
Food from Russia and the Caucasus.
Kalinka-Stockmann
Smolenskaya Ploshchad 3/5. Tel: 785
2500. www.stockmann.ru. Metro:
Smolenskaya.
Deli and supermarket in the Smolenskiy
Passazh arcade; takes Mastercard and Visa.
Novoarbatskiy
Noviy Arbat 13. Tel: 291 5828. Metro:
Arbatskaya/Smolenskaya. Open: 24/7.
Credit cards.

Ramstore Krasnaya
Presnya 23b. www.ramstore.ru.
Metro: Ulitsa 1905 Goda. Open: 24/7.

St Petersburg:
Kalinka-Stockmann
Finlyandskiy Prospekt 1. Tel: 542 2297.
www.stockmann.ru. Metro: Ploshchad
Lenina. Takes all cards.

SHOPPING CENTRES
Moscow:
Atrium
Zemlyanoy Val 33. Metro: Kurskaya.
Galereya Aktyor
Tverskaya 16/2. Tel: 290 9832. Metro:
Pushkinskaya.
GUM
Krasnaya Ploshchad 3. Tel: 921 5763.
www.gum.ru. Metro: Ploshchad Revolyutsii.
Okhotniy Ryad
Manezhnaya Ploshchad 1. Tel: 737 8449.
www.okhot-ryad.ru. Metro: Okhotniy
Ryad.
Petrovskiy Passazh
Petrovka 10. Tel: 928 5047. Metro:
Teatralnaya.
TsUM
Petrovka 2. Tel: 292 1157. www.tsum.ru.
Metro: Teatralnaya.

St Petersburg
Gostiniy Dvor
Nevskiy Prospekt 35. Metro: Nevskiy
Prospekt/Gostiniy Dvor. An 18th-century
bazaar, now a shopping mall.
Grand Palace
Nevskiy Prospekt 44. Metro: Nevskiy
Prospekt/Gostiniy Dvor.
Passazh
Nevskiy Prospekt 48. Metro: Nevskiy
Prospekt/Gostiniy Dvor.

The market – *rynok* – is a central element of city life in Moscow and St Petersburg. Somehow, these strongholds of small-scale capitalism managed to survive communism's assault on private property. This was not least, perhaps, because even the most dutiful party functionary relied on the markets for that little something special when the shelves of the state shops were barren of all but a few wizened beetroot and dusty jars of pickled cucumbers.

Moscow's Cheryomushinskiy or St Petersburg's

Kuznechniy markets are an experience in themselves, a microcosm of the old Soviet Union. Traders from all corners of the former empire accost the casual visitor: swarthy Georgians proffer bright red roses 'for the beautiful lady, sir'; Uzbeks and Turkmen crouch over piles of watermelons and sacks of roasted sunflower seeds; buxom Ukrainians invite you to try their national favourite – huge slabs of pork fat called *salo*; fishermen from the Caspian Sea stand proudly in front of bucketfuls of red and black caviar; and old ladies in bright headscarves sell salted tomatoes and pickled garlic from their allotments in the suburbs of the city.

Some of the goods are as exotic as the salespeople, ranging from whole sturgeons and beluga whales to Armenian brandies and *kvas*, Russia's traditional black bread beer. The meat section is not for the squeamish, with cuts that have long disappeared from Western supermarkets – pig's trotters, goats' heads, complete ox tongues and internal organs best left unnamed. And, for refreshment, there is sure to be a bottle of the country's lethal moonshine, *samogon*, discreetly hidden under the counter.

The welcome is warm and the sales patter persuasive. Little has changed since the 19th century when a foreign traveller noted that the stallholders in Russia's markets have, 'notwithstanding their lust of gain, a cheerfulness of temperament wholly wanting to the German or the English merchant'.

Opposite above and below: Russian markets offer anything ranging from food ... to icons ...
Below: ... to Christmas decorations

Entertainment

No trip to Russia is quite complete without an evening at the legendary Bolshoy Theatre in Moscow or St Petersburg's world-famous Mariinskiy Theatre, still sometimes known by its Soviet name, the Kirov. But as befits one of the world's great cultures, entertainment possibilities are virtually endless and there is sure to be something to suit everyone.

Entertainment is never too far away

What's on

Planning your time amid the wealth of entertainment on offer is probably the greatest problem for culture-hungry visitors to Russia. Members of package tours may find that a trip to the Bolshoy or Mariinskiy is already included in their schedule, simplifying the decision-making process. Otherwise, the best sources of information are the various entertainments listings.

Most convenient are the inserts printed periodically in the English-language newspapers distributed free of charge in Western-style hotels, bars and foreign-run supermarkets. The *Moscow Times, www.themoscow.times.com* and *Moscow Tribune, www.tribune.ru*, publish exhaustive listings in their pages every Friday. The former also prints on the back page a short daily 'What is to be done?' column listing the evening's highlights. Similar listings are available for St Petersburg in *Pulse* magazine, *www.pulse.ru* and the *St Petersburg Times, www.sptimes.ru*.

Most hotels have a service bureau which will inform you of current events or group trips organised by local tour agencies or by the hotel itself.

Failing any of the above you will have to decipher the Russian-language posters pasted at strategic positions on the streets, hung in the windows of ticket kiosks throughout the town (*see below*) or advertised outside the venues.

Tickets

The best way of obtaining tickets is to contact one of the agencies mentioned below. Alternatively, try the service bureaux in the hotels, but give them as much notice as possible as tickets sell out quickly. Where major venues are concerned, a two-tier pricing policy operates to ensure that Westerners pay inflated prices. While it is theoretically possible to buy face-value tickets at box offices, you will find it virtually impossible to get into the venue unless you can pass as a Russian. Theatre booking offices have seating plans to help you choose your ticket. *Traveller's Yellow Pages* to Moscow and St Petersburg also print seating plans for major venues. If all else fails, you can try haggling with the ticket touts who hang around entrances an hour or two before performances. Be sure to check the date and seat number before you buy.

Most performances begin at 7pm.

TICKET AGENCIES
Moscow:
IPC
(Metropol Hotel) Teatralniy Proezd 1/4.
Tel: 927 6982.
Kontramarka
Tel: 933 3200. www.kontramarka.ru
Parter
Tel: 258 0000. www.parter.ru

St Petersburg:
Mariinskiy Ticket Office
Gostiniy Dvor Branch. Tel: 326 4141.
www.mariinsky.ru
Sofit
Ploshchad Dekabristov 35. Tel: 327 7400.
www.sofit.spb.ru
All tickets.
Vizit
Italyianskaya 10. Tel: 310 5136.
www.russianballet.spb.ru
For ballet performances in the
Aleksandrinskiy Theatre.

CINEMAS
Moscow:
5 Zvezd (5 Stars)
Bakhrushina 25. Tel: 953 4206.
www.5zvezd.ru. Metro: Paveletskaya.
Huge four-storey complex, with waterfall,
bars, glass lift, chill-out amphitheatre,
offers film hits of the season.
35 mm
Pokrovka 47/24. Tel: 917 5492. Metro:
Kurskaya/Krasnye Vorota.
Non-stop shows of European, Asian and
American alternative cinematography.
America-Cinema
Berezhkovskaya Naberezhnaya 2,
Radisson Slavyanskaya Hotel, 2nd floor.

Tel: 941 8895, 941 8747. www.america-
cinema.ru. Metro: Kievskaya.
Cinema favourite among foreigners, who
can view all box-office hits in English.
Formula Kino
Zemlyanoy Val 33. Tel: 795 3795.
www.imperiakino.ru. Metro: Kurskaya.
This two-storey cinema complex has
nine screens. It offers, like almost all
Moscow's cinemas, hits made elsewhere.
Gorizont (Horizon)
Komsomolskiy Prospekt 21/10. Tel: 245
3143. www.imperiakino.ru. Metro:
Frunzenskaya.
Visitors sit comfortably in adjustable seats
while watching films from the A-list.
Kinotsentr (Cinema Centre)
Druzhinnikovskaya 15. Tel: 255 9057.
www.kinocenter.ru. Metro:
Krasnopresnenskaya.
If you missed any films of the past
season, you can usually catch them here.
Praga (Prague)
Nizhnaya Maslovka 10. Tel: 795 3795.
www.imperiakino.ru. Metro:
Savyolovskaya.
This huge cinema is a favourite among
children, but adults in search of new
releases should pay it a visit too.
Pushkinskiy (Pushkin's Cinema)
Pushkinskaya Ploshchad 2. Tel: 795 3795.
Metro: Pushkinskaya.
Very large cinema, whose huge screen is
great for Hollywood blockbusters.

St Petersburg:
Aurora Cinema
Nevskiy Prospekt 60. Tel: 315 5254.
www.avrora.spb.ru
Crystal Palace
Nevskiy Prospekt 72. Tel: 272 2382.
www.cp.spb.ru

З июня

Лучано Паваротти

UNIVERSAL заказ билетов 995-95-20, 933-33-88

Russia is frequently visited by the world's best-known and most popular stars

Dom Kino
ul Karavannaya 12. Tel: 314 0638.
www.domkino.spb.ru
Mirazh (Mirage) Cinema
Bolshoy Prospekt, Petrogradskaya side 35.
Tel: 238 0758. www.mirage.ru

Clubs and Casinos
Russia's *nouveaux riches* either make their money or spend it at the profusion of brand-new nightclubs and casinos whose neon lights illuminate the main streets of Moscow and St Petersburg after dark. Moscow is reputedly rivalled in number of casinos only by Las Vegas!

More tasteful than their Soviet-era counterparts, they often boast fashion shows, restaurants and Western DJs in addition to the dancing and gaming. They can be a little disconcerting for the uninitiated. Be prepared to be thoroughly searched for firearms by beefy guards on entry (some clubs even have special lockers for their safe keeping). Some charge a hefty entrance fee and nearly

all demand a reasonable standard of dress (jacket and tie for men).

The quality and safety of any of the places mentioned below can vary drastically in a short time, largely depending on whether or not it has been adopted by one of the local mafia groups.

On leaving, you will find that taxis are a lot cheaper if you walk a few blocks away from the club entrance.

The more popular destinations in Moscow include the following:
B2
This rock and pop club is a branch of the Moscow club, Bunker. Its five floors of entertainment make it the biggest club in Moscow. Dancing and live concerts.
Bolshaya Sadovaya 8. Tel: 209 9918, 209 9909. Open: daily noon–6am. Admission charge. Metro: Mayakovskaya.
B B King
Food, live jazz/blues music, visitors may join in playing instruments.
Sadovaya-Samotetchnaya 4/2. Tel: 299 8206. www.bibiking.ru. Open: daily noon–2am. No admission charge except Sat. Metro: Tsvetnoi Bulvar.
Bunker
Eating, dancing and rock concerts.
Tverskaya Ulitsa 12. Tel: 941 9515. www.bunker.ru. Open: non-stop. Admission charge. Metro: Pushkinskaya.
Garazh
Dancing, restaurant, striptease.
Tverskaya 16. Tel: 209 1848. Open: non-stop. No admission charge. Metro: Pushkinskaya.
JVL Art Club
Nightly jazz, folk, even classical shows with a touch of retro.

Novoslobodskaya 14/19. Tel: 978 9115.
www.jvlartclub.jazz.ru. Closed: Sun.
Metro: Novoslobodskaya.

Karma-Bar

Lively and fairly relaxed bar and dance
floor with varied programme of parties,
DJs, R&B, soul etc.
Pushechnaya 3. Tel: 924 5633.
www.karma-bar.ru. Metro: Lubyanka/
Kuznetskiy most.

Kino (Cinema)

Club restaurant, frequented by
personalities from the film industry.
Call ahead to reserve a table.
Olimpiyskiy Prospekt 16. Tel: 974 2533.
www.kino-club.ru. Open: Mon–Wed, Fri
noon–2am, Sat 5pm–2am.
No admission charge. Metro: Prospekt
Mira.

Le Club

Jazz club, live music.
V Radishchevskaya 21. Tel: 915 1042.
Open: daily noon–midnight. Admission
charge. Metro: Taganskaya.

Metelitsa

Dancing, casino, restaurant.
Noviy Arbat 21. Tel: 291 1170.
www.metelitsa.ru. Open: Mon–Thur
9pm–5am, Fri–Sat 9pm–6am.
Admission charge. Metro: Arbatskaya.

Petrovich

Restaurant, dancing, concerts.
Myasnitskaya 24. Tel: 923 0082. Open:
daily noon–6am. Admission charge.
Metro: Tchistiye Prudi.

R&B Café

Located in the very centre. Live music,
dancing, concerts.
Starovagankovskiy Pereulok 19. Tel: 203
6008. Open: noon–midnight.
Admission charge. Metro: Biblioteka im
Lenina.

St Petersburg has fewer top-quality
nightspots, but new ones are being
advertised all the time:

Café Club Che

Live music nightly with a sophisticated
Cuban beat.
Poltavskaya 3. Tel: 277 7600. Metro:
Ploshchad Aleksandra
Nevskovo/Ploshchad Vostaniya.

Griboyedov Club

Open every night, this club offers a wide
range of live music from rock to jazz.
Voronezhskaya 2a. Tel: 164 4355. Metro:
Ligovskiy Prospekt.

Hollywood Nites

Nightclub and casino with disco at
weekends.
Nevskiy Prospekt 46. Tel: 311 6077/325
7474. Metro: Nevskiy Prospekt/Gostiniy
Dvor.

Club Plaza

Nightclub, restaurant and casino.
Nab Makarova 2. Tel: 323 9090.
www.plazaclub.ru. Metro:
Vasileostrovskaya.

Premier Casino

Casino and restaurant in historic
building.
Nevskiy Prospekt 47. Tel: 103 5370.
www.clubpremier.ru

Red Club

This interesting venue continues to
attract journalists and musicians with its
eclectic programme.
Poltavskaya 7. Tel: 277 1366/0000.
www.clubred.ru. Metro: Ploshchad
Aleksandra Nevskovo/Ploshchad Vostaniya.

Red Fox Jazz Club

Refreshingly relaxed and informal, this
café specialises in live trad-jazz.
Mayakovskovo 50. Tel: 275 4214.
www.rfjc.ru. Metro: Chernyshevskaya.

Music and Theatre

You can find a world-class orchestra or ballet troupe performing on practically any day of the season in Moscow or St Petersburg (most concert halls are closed throughout July and August), and many venues host folk dance and music from every corner of Russia.

It is sometimes better to book ahead …

CLASSICAL MUSIC

Check in advance – when the Bolshoy and Mariinskiy companies are on tour, their theatres house visiting companies.

Moscow concert venues:
Dvorets Syezdov (State Kremlin Palace)
Kreml. Tel: 917 2336. Metro: Aleksandrovskiy Sad or Borovitskaya.
Moscow Conservatory
Includes two halls – *bolshoy* (large) and *maliy* (small) *zal.*
Ulitsa Bolshaya Nikitskaya 13. Tel: 229 7412/9436. www.moscons.ru. Metro: Okhotniy Ryad.
Rossiya Concert Hall
In the Rossiya Hotel complex.
Moskvoretskaya Naberezhnaya 1. Tel: 298 4350. Metro: Ploshchad Revolyutsii.
Tchaikovsky Concert Hall
Home of the State Symphony Orchestra.
4/31 Triumfalnaya Ploshchad. Tel: 299 3681/299 0378. www.philharmonia.ru. Metro: Mayakovskaya.

St Petersburg concert venues:
Akademicheskaya Kapella (Academic Capella)
Offers choral music and small ensembles.
Naberezhnaya Reki Moyki 20. Tel: 314 1058. Metro: Nevskiy Prospekt.

Beloselskiy-Belozerskiy Palace
Here the St Petersburg City Concert Orchestra performs in the glittering surroundings of the palace ballroom.
Nevskiy Prospekt 41. Tel: 315 5235. (Box office noon–6pm.) Metro: Gostiniy Dvor.
Filarmoniya (St Petersburg Philharmonia)
Mikhailovskaya Ulitsa 2 (big hall), Nevskiy Prospekt 30 (smaller Glinka hall). Tel: 110 4257/311 8333 respectively. www.philharmonia.spb.ru. Metro: Nevskiy Prospekt.
Oktyabrskiy Concert Hall
Ligovskiy Prospekt 6. Tel: 275 1300/1310. www.reserve.sp.ru/bkz. Metro: Ploshchad Vosstaniya.

OPERA AND BALLET

Moscow:
Bolshoy Theatre
Almost 1,000 individuals make up the combined opera and ballet companies of the Bolshoy, but with dwindling state subsidies forcing ever more tours you will be lucky to catch them.
Teatralnaya Ploshchad 1. Tel: 292 9986/ 0050. www.bolshoi.ru. Metro: Teatralnaya Ploshchad. Main theatre currently closed for repairs. Performances take place on the New Stage (see p153).

Dvorets Syezdov (State Kremlin Palace)
Home to the State Classical Ballet
Theatre. See **Classical Music** for details.

St Petersburg:
Ermitazhniy Teatr (Hermitage Theatre)
Dvortsovaya nab 32. Tel: 279 0226.
Mariinskiy Theatre
Also known as the Kirov, the Mariinskiy's
reputations are undiminished.
Teatralnaya Ploshchad 1. Tel: 326 4141.
Metro: Sadovaya.
Mussorgsky Opera and Ballet Theatre
Ploshchad Iskusstv 1. Tel: 219 1978.
Metro: Nevskiy Prospekt.

JAZZ, ROCK AND POP
Russia today has a vibrant rock and jazz
scene, and both cities offer the full
range, from smoke-filled jazz clubs and
underground hard rock dens to full-
scale concerts. Ever more foreign stars
are including Russia on their European
tours; the English-language press carries
announcements well in advance.
   Phone ahead for current opening
times (usually Friday and weekend
evenings) or see press for concert details.

Moscow's favourite venues
(*see also pp148–9*):
Arbat Blues Club
Aksakov Pereulok 11. Tel: 291 1546.
Metro: Arbatskaya.
The Bunker Club
Rock and pop.
Tverskaya 12. Tel: 209 4470.
www.bunker.ru. Metro: Tverskaya.
Tabula Rasa
Rock concerts and DJ sets.
Berezhkovskaya Naberezhnaya 38.
Tel: 240 9289. Metro: Kievskaya.

St Petersburg (*see also pp148–9*):
Dzhaz filarmonik kholl
(Jazz Philharmonic Hall)
Zagorodniy Prospekt 27. Tel: 164 8565.
www.jazz-hall.spb.ru/engl.html
Griboyedov
Voronezhskaya Ulitsa 2A. Tel: 164 4355.
JFC Jazz Club
Shpalernaya Ulitsa 33. Tel: 272 9850.
www.jfc.spb.ru. Metro: Chernyshevskaya.
Metro
Ligovskiy Prospekt 174. Tel: 166
0211/0210. www.metroclub.ru

THEATRE

Moscow:
Chekhov Moscow Art Theatre (MKhAT)
Kamergerskiy Pereulok 3. Tel: 229 8760.
Metro: Teatralnaya Ploshchad.
Maliy Theatre
Teatralnaya Ploshchad 1/6. Tel: 923 2621.
Metro: Teatralnaya Ploshchad.
Lenkom Theatre
Malaya Dmitrovka 6. Tel: 299 0708.
Metro: Pushkinskaya/Chekhovskaya.
Taganka Theatre
Zemlyanoy val 76. Tel: 915 1217.
www.taganka.org. Metro: Taganskaya.

St Petersburg:
Aleksandriinskiy Theatre
Ploshchad Ostrovskoyo 2. Tel: 110
4103/312 1545. Metro: Nevskiy
Prospekt/Gostiniy Dvor.
Bolshoy Drama Theatre (BDT)
Reki Fontanki Naberezhnaya 65. Tel: 310
9242/0401. Metro: Sennaya Ploshchad.
Maliy Drama Theatre
Ulitsa Rubinshteyna 18. Tel: 113 2078.
www.mdt-dodin.ru. Metro:
Vladimirskaya.

The Bolshoy

The origins of Moscow's greatest ballet and opera company, the Bolshoy, date back to 1776 when the Moscow procurator, Prince Urusov, formed the first permanent Russian theatre company from the serfs on his estate. They performed in the mansion of his friend Count Vorontsov before the company was established, four years later, as the Petrovskiy Theatre on the site at the end of Ulitsa Petrovka where it remains today.

The monumental classical building that dominates Teatralnaya Ploshchad is the third Bolshoy Theatre. The first burned down in 1805, as did its successor in 1853. The final version outdoes London's Covent Garden and Milan's La Scala in sheer scale, and is celebrated for its superb acoustics; as the architect remarked: 'It is built like a musical instrument.'

Many great Russian works, most famously Tchaikovsky's ballet *Swan Lake*, were premiered at the Bolshoy, but it was not until Soviet times, with Moscow again the capital, that it emerged from the shadow of St Petersburg's Mariinskiy Theatre, better known as the Kirov. During the Bolshoy's modern heyday in the 1960s and 1970s, opera houses around the world were packed with audiences mesmerised by the company's performances of Stravinsky's *Petrushka* and Khachaturian's *Gayane* with its breathtaking 'Sabre Dance'.

Those days are over. The Bolshoy's repertoire has been cut along with once lavish state subsidies, and top dancers are loaned abroad to raise

much-needed funds. Each season is punctuated by pay disputes and strikes by the company's 900 members. A long-standing feud was brought to a head in 1995 when the much-loved artistic director resigned after a battle with theatre authorities; the dancers promptly walked out of a performance in protest. When they appeared in court a few days later, the capital was left to wonder how long the flagship of Russia's 200-year-old ballet tradition would survive into the 21st century.

The Bolshoy is currently going through its 230th season employing more than 2,500 people. Many world-famous opera singers have performed on its stage – Monserrat Caballe, Luciano Pavarotti, Jose Carreras and many others. It also regularly holds performances by theatres from Germany, Sweden, the USA and many other countries. While the Bolshoy is closed for repairs, performances will take place on the New Stage next door. *www.bolshoi.ru*

The Bolshoy – in all its glory

National Holidays and Festivals

Today new holidays marking turning points in the struggle against Soviet power take their place alongside resurrected religious festivals in the Orthodox calendar. Landmarks in Bolshevik history that were once solemnly celebrated are now low-key events. Both Moscow and St Petersburg host a series of annual arts and music festivals.

Russian dancers in traditional costumes

December/January

December 25–January 5: **Russian Winter festival**. A secular celebration with family parties and cultural programmes at the two cities' main venues (*see pp150–1*). **New Year's Day** (January 1) is Russia's foremost holiday, with present-giving by Ded-Moroz, 'Grandfather Frost' (*see p136*).

January 7: **Orthodox Christmas**, with all-night liturgies in church.

January 13/14: **Orthodox New Year** – not officially a holiday but treated as such.

January 27: **Breaking of the Siege of Leningrad**. A public holiday in St Petersburg.

February/March

February 23: **Defenders of the Motherland Day**. The successor of Red Army Day, no longer a national holiday, but still the occasion of public drinking parties.

February/March: **Maslenitsa**, marking the end of winter and the beginning of Lent. Not a public holiday but celebrated by huge feasting (see *p136*).

February 19–March 5: **Farewell to Russian Winter** festival in St Petersburg.

Sleigh rides and traditional food, costumes and dancing, based at the Olgino campsite (*18km (11 miles) along Primorskoe Shosse. Tel: 238 3552*).

March 8: **International Women's Day**. A day off for everybody except city flower-sellers.

March/April

Easter, *paskha*, is the chief Orthodox festival. Children colour eggs and enjoy the traditional dish of sweetened curds with raisins, also called *paskha*. *www.easterfestival.ru*

April/May

End of April/early May: **Musical Spring** festival in St Petersburg. International concerts at the city's main venues (*see pp150–1*).

May/June

May 1/2: **International Working People's Solidarity Day**. A day for demonstrations by communists and a holiday for everyone else.

May 9: **Victory Day**. Celebrates the end of the Soviet Union's participation in World War II. Parades and wreath-

laying in Moscow's Park Pobedy and at the Tomb of the Unknown Soldier, and processions of veterans along Nevskiy Prospekt in St Petersburg.
June 12: **Russian Independence Day**. Commemorates Russia's secession from the Soviet Union in 1991.

June/July
June 21–July 1: **White Nights** festival in St Petersburg. Long nights celebrating the summer solstice when the sun virtually never sets. Informal partying on the streets, plus concerts on Yelagin Island (*metro Chernaya Rechka, then overland transport heading down Primorskiy Prospekt to the bridge*). Crowds gather on the river embankment to watch the bridges being raised just after 1.30am.

August/September
First four days of August: **Love Street Festival** in Moscow. Off-beat street entertainments and fringe art around

Pokrovskiy Bulvar (*metro: Chistiye Prudy*) and in Moscow's clubs (*see pp148–9*).
September 6 (or nearest Sat): **Moscow City Day**. Parade and festivities.
September 8: **Siege of Leningrad Day**. Not a public holiday, but a day of mourning and remembrance in St Petersburg.
Late Sept early Oct (Moscow): **Solomon Mikoels International Festival**. Drama, music, film and literature.

October/November
November 7 (October 25 by old Russian calendar): **Revolution Day**. Once celebrated by the Soviet arsenal rolling across Red Square and now marked (unofficially) by communist marches.
Mid-November: **Autumn Rhythms** jazz festival in St Petersburg, centred on the city's jazz clubs (*see p151*).
Autumn (odd years only): **Moscow Film Festival** *www.miff.ru* (see English-language press for details).

Despite their hardships in life, Russians know how to enjoy themselves

Children

Snowstorms and sledging make the Russian winter fun for children of all ages, but even in the summer months Moscow and St Petersburg have plenty to keep youngsters interested.

There are many places for children to enjoy themselves

MOSCOW
Delphinari (Dolphinarium)
In Moscow's Palace of Water Sports (Dvorets Vodnovo Sporta), dolphins, seals and a beluga whale called Yegor are guaranteed to delight on a rainy day. *Ulitsa Mironovskaya 27. Tel: 369 7966. Shows: Times vary, but are approximately 2 hourly from noon–6pm. Admission charge. Metro: Semyonovskaya, Izmaylovskiy Park.*

ST PETERSBURG
Bassein Spartak
Konstantinovskiy Pr 19. Tel: 235 4631. Metro: Krestovskiy Ostrov.

Some attractions may even be enjoyed by the parents

Museums
Those in Moscow likely to appeal to youngsters include the Borodino Battle Panorama and the Space Travel, Armed Forces and Polytechnic museums (*see pp54–7*).

Life-size effigies of Russia's good, bad and ugly in Moscow's waxworks exhibition appeal to children of all ages. *Tverskaya Ulitsa 14. Tel: 229 8552. Open: Wed–Sun 11am–7pm; Tue 11am–6pm. Closed: Mon. Metro: Mayakovskaya.*

In St Petersburg, Peter the Great's extraordinary Kunstkammer (Museum of Anthropology and Ethnography – *see p110*) will capture any teenager's imagination. The Historical Waxworks in the Stroganovskiy Palace, the Ethnographic and Naval museums (*see pp110–11*), as well as the *Aurora* Cruiser (*see p110*), may also prove popular.

Parks
Russian amusement parks have a long way to go if they want to rival Euro-Disney, but what they lack in hi-tech rides is made up for by the holiday atmosphere and low fares.

Park im A M Gorkovo (Gorky Park) in the centre of Moscow boasts a roller coaster, boating lake and magnificent Ferris wheel.

Krymskiy Val Ulitsa 9. Tel: 237 0707.
Metro: Park Kultury Oktyabrskaya.

In St Petersburg: **Central Park of Culture and Rest**
Elagin Ostrov 4. Tel: 430 0911. Metro: Krestovskiy Ostrov.

River Rides
A cruise in a motor launch among the canals of St Petersburg restores the culture-sated, young or old (*see p138*). Hydrofoil and pleasure boat trips tour the Moscow river in warmer months. You can board at several locations, but the most convenient are next to Kievskaya Vokzal (Kievskiy railway station) and on the embankment at Gorky Park.

THEATRE AND CIRCUS
Puppet theatres are a well-loved Russian tradition, and even though the shows are in Russian, smaller children will be fascinated.
Moscow:
Obraztsov Puppet Theatre
Sadovaya-Samotyochnaya Ulitsa 3. Tel: 299 5373. www.puppet.ru. Metro: Mayakovskaya.

St Petersburg:
Bryantsev Theatre for Young Viewers
Pionerskaya pl 1. Tel: 112 4172. Metro: Pushkinskaya.
Demmeni Puppet Theatre
52 Nevskiy Prospekt. Tel: 117 2156. Metro: Moskovskie Vorota.

No trip to Russia is complete without a visit to the circus. The shows are spectacular, with animals, Cossack acrobats and the world's best clowns.

Moscow:
State Circus (Tsirk Nikulina)
Much improved with acts from all over the world; thoroughly entertaining.
Tsvetnoy Bulvar 13. Tel: 200 0668. Metro: Tsvetnoy Bulvar.

St Petersburg:
Circus on Fontanka
Nab reki Fontanki 3. Tel: 314 8478. www.circus.spb.ru. Metro: Gostiniy Dvor.

Views of the City
Some of the best views of Moscow are from Sparrow Hills (*Metro: Universitet/ Vorobvovie Gory*) where there is woodland for the children to run around in. The roof-top panoramas from St Isaac's Cathedral in St Petersburg are breathtaking (*see p108*).

Zoos
Moscow and St Petersburg zoos must rank as two of the least attractive in the world. Nevertheless, most children are likely to spend a perfectly happy summer's afternoon wandering among the polar bears and popcorn sellers.
Moskovskiy Zoopark (Moscow Zoo)
Bolshaya Gruzinskaya Ulitsa 1. Tel: 255 6034. Open: Tue–Sun 10am–8pm (summer); 10am–5pm (winter). Admission charge. Metro: Barrikadnaya, Krasnopresnenskaya.
Zoopark ('Leningrad' Zoo)
Local commercial interests and their political allies want to develop this land – catch it whilst you can!
Aleksandrovskiy Park 1. Tel: 232 8260. www.spbzoo.ru. Open: 10am–7pm summer; 10am–5pm winter. Closed: Mon. Admission charge. Metro: Gorkovskaya.

Sport

As one of the world's greatest sporting nations, Russia has a lot to offer sports fans of almost every persuasion. You can enjoy first-rate football and ice hockey matches for a fraction of the cost at home, and there is ample opportunity to get involved yourself – from skiing and skating to hunting wild boar or flying a Soviet jet! And at the end of the day, you can treat yourself to a Russian steam bath.

Take a dip in the cold sea …

BATHHOUSES

Getting steamed up at the *banya* is not so much a way of getting clean as a whole Russian subculture in itself. *Cognoscenti* of the *banya* do not expect to spend less than three hours relaxing in the hot and cold rooms, playing pool, working out, philosophising and drinking beer – all, of course, completely nude.

Remember to take your own towel, toiletries and sandals. Birch twig *veniki*, for mutual exfoliation, are sold on the premises. Sexes strictly segregated.

… or relax in hot bathhouses

Moscow:
Sandunovskiye Banyi
The best *banya* by far, their elegant décor making them a sight in themselves.
Neglinnaya Pereulok 14.
Tel: 925 4631. www.sandung.ru.
Metro: Kuznetskiy Most.

St Petersburg:
Yamskiye Banyi
Dostoevskovo 9. Tel: 312 5836.
Closed: Tue. Metro: Vladimirskaya.

BOWLING ALLEYS
Moscow:
Aurora
Profsoyuznaya 154. Tel: 339 4187.
Open: daily 11am–5am.
Metro: Tyopliy Stan.
Bi-Ba-Bo
Karmanitskiy Pereulok 9. Tel: 937 4337.
Open: daily 3pm–5am. Metro:
Smolenskaya.
Champion
The largest in the city, with 20 lanes, also pool and snooker, big-screen TV, eating facilities and bars.
Leningradskoe shosse 16. Tel: 747 5000.
www.champion.ru. Open 7 days. Metro:
Voykovskaya.

St Petersburg:
Aquatoria *Vyborgskaya* 159
Naberezhnaya 61. Tel: 245 2030.
Metro: Vyborgskaya.
Cosmic Bowling
Aptekarskiy Prospekt, 16. Tel: 234 4935.
Metro: Petrogradskaya.

CROSS-COUNTRY SKIING
Flat terrain rules out downhill skiing
but the cross-country variety is hugely
popular. Head for any of the outlying
parks in winter. Skis can be acquired at
most sports shops for a modest outlay
(*see p143*).

GOLF
Popular with Moscow's image-
conscious *nouveaux riches*, the up-
market **Tumba Golf Club** also accepts
green fees.
Ulitsa Dovzhenko 1. Tel: 147 6254.
Metro: Universitet, then bus 67 to
Ulitsa Mosfilmovskaya.

HORSE RACING
Risk a few roubles betting on fast-action
buggy racing in the centre of Moscow
on Wednesdays and weekends at the
Hippodrome.
Ulitsa Begovaya 22. Tel: 945 0437.
Metro: Begovaya.

HORSE RIDING
It is hard to beat the romance of riding
through birch forests in springtime or
taking a horse-drawn sleigh ride after
a fresh snowfall.
Moscow:
Bittsa Horse Riding Complex
The riding school in this pleasant park
on the outskirts of the city offers lessons

at all levels. Other facilities include a
gym and swimming pool.
Balaklavskiy Prospekt 33. Tel: 318 5744.
Open: Mon–Fri 9am–9pm, Sat–Sun
9am–6pm. Metro: Kaluzhskaya, then bus
28 or 624.

St Petersburg:
Prostor Park stables organise pony
riding and sleigh rides.
Krestovskiy Prospekt 22. Tel: 230 7873.
Metro: Krestovskiy Ostrov.

HUNTING
The 55,000-hectare (135,900-acre)
Ozerinskoe Reserve outside Moscow
was former Soviet leader Leonid
Brezhnev's favourite hunting ground.
A well-kept lodge includes a restaurant
which will roast the results of the day's
sport in the evening. For hunting trips
see: *www.hunting.in-Russia.com*

ICE HOCKEY
When it is too cold for football, passions
switch to ice hockey, played at world
standard in Russia's two big cities.
International matches are advertised in
the local press. Tickets at stadiums.
Moscow:
Moscow's soccer teams (*see pp160–1*)
all have corresponding hockey squads,
of which the Krilya Sovetov is the best.
They play at Krilya Ice Palace.
Tolbukhina 10/3. Tel: 448 8777. Metro:
Kuntsevskaya, then bus 179.

St Petersburg:
Ledoviy Dvorets (Ice Palace)
1 Pyatiletok Prospekt. Tel: 118 6620.
www.newarena.spb.ru. Metro: Prospekt
Bolshevikov.

Sign outside the Dinamo sports club in
St Petersburg

ICE SKATING

You can skate the icy boulevards of
Moscow's Gorky Park in winter or visit
one of many covered rinks. Some places
hire out skates, but bring extra pairs of
socks in case your size is not available.

Moscow:

Gorky Park

The rink turns into a disco on ice in the
evenings. Skate hire available.
Krymskiy Val Ulitsa 9. Tel: 237 0713/1350.
Metro: Park Kultury.

Sokolniki Palace of Sports

Three indoor rinks.
Sokolnicheskiy Val 16. Tel: 268 6958.
Metro: Sokolniki.

Stadion unikh pionerov

Leningradskiy Prospekt 31. Tel: 213 4642.
Open: 24 hours daily. Metro: Dinamo.

St Petersburg:

Yubileiniy Palace of Sports

Skate hire available.
Prospekt Dobrolyubova 18. Tel: 323 9315.
Metro: Sportivnaya.

JOGGING

Moscow's expatriate community gathers
at 2pm outside the Ukraine Hotel on
Sundays all year round for the Hash
House Harriers' run around the city.
Lighthearted fun with ritual beer
drinking at the end. Contact your
embassy for details.
Kutuzovskiy Prospekt 2/1. Metro: Kievskaya.

SAILING

The following centres offer leisure
yachting in the summer months, but call
ahead to confirm availability.

Moscow:

Spartak Yacht Club charters yachts and
instructors on an hourly rate and can
arrange longer trips to St Petersburg or
Astrakhan on the Volga delta.
*Dolgoprudniy Town, Naberezhnaya Ulitsa
4a. Tel: 408 2500, 576 0202.*
*www.spartak.ws. 5km along Dimitrovskoe
Shosse or by elektrichka from Savyolovskiy
Vokzal.*

St Petersburg:

Neva Yacht Club organises sailing in the
Gulf of Finland and can also supply
motorboats.
Naberezhnaya Martynova 94,
Krestovskiy Island. Tel: 235 2722.
Metro: Krestovskiy Ostrov.

SOCCER

Russians adore soccer, and do so
with a refreshing lack of European-style

hooliganism. Tickets are always available for local matches on the day at the stadium. The season is from March to October.

Moscow:

Moscow's chief soccer teams, Torpedo, Dinamo and CSKA, play respectively at:

Sportivnaya Arena Luzhniki (Luzhniki Stadium)

Luzhnetskaya Naberezhnaya 24. Tel: 201 1164. Metro: Sportivnaya.

Stadion Dinamo (Dinamo Stadium)

Leningradskiy Prospekt 36. Tel: 213 3766. www.fcdinamo.ru. Metro: Dinamo.

Stadion TsSKA

Leningradskiy Prospekt 39. Tel: 213 6592. Metro: Aeroport.

St Petersburg:

Zenit FC plays at **Petrovskiy Stadium** (Kirov Stadium) on Petrovskiy Island.

Morskoy Prospekt 1. Tel: 119 5701. www.zenit.spb.org. Metro: Sportivnaya.

SWIMMING

Many hotels have swimming pools on the premises. If yours does not, ask at your hotel reception for the nearest pool, or alternatively try the following.

Moscow:

Olympic Sports Complex

Olympiyskiy Prospekt 18. Tel: 288 1533. Open: 7am–6pm Mon–Fri. Metro: Prospekt Mira.

Radisson Slavyanskaya Hotel

Berezhkovskaya Naberezhnaya 2. Tel: 941 8000/20. www.radissonmoscow.ru. Metro: Kievskaya.

St Petersburg:

Dinamo Sports Centre

(see below).

TENNIS

Tennis is a boom sport in Russia and the country's best compete against foreign stars in Moscow's Kremlin Cup. See local press for details. You can also have a few sets yourself at the following venues.

Moscow:

Dinamo Centr

Petrovka 26. Tel: 200 5836. Open: daily, outdoor 7am–9pm, indoor 7am–midnight. Metro: Okhotniy Ryad/Teatralnaya.

Luzhniki

Luzhnetskaya Naberezhnaya 24.

Tel: 201 0794. Open: daily 7am–11pm. Metro: Sportivnaya.

St Petersburg:

Dinamo

A mix of courts (book ahead).

Prospekt Dinamo 44. Tel: 235 4717. Metro: Krestovskiy Ostrov.

WORKOUT

Both Moscow and St Petersburg have good selections of well-equipped gyms.

Moscow:

Chaika Sport Complex

Turchaninov Pereulok 1/3. Tel: 246 1344. Metro: Park Kultury.

Fit Olimp

Olympiyskiy Prospekt 16. Tel: 688 2088. Metro: Prospekt Mira.

St Petersburg:

Neptune Hotel

Gym, swimming pool, sauna, solarium, Turkish bath, aerobics classes.

Naberezhnaya Obvodnovo Kanala 93a. Tel: 324 4696/4610. Metro: Pushkinskaya.

Planet Fitness

in Grand Hotel Europe, Mikhaylovskaya Ulitsa 1/7. Tel: 329 6597.

Food and Drink

As market reforms continue to bite, Russia is rapidly overcoming its once well-deserved reputation as a gastronomic disaster area. In Moscow and St Petersburg at least, the days of barely edible food and appalling service are all but a distant memory and the hungry traveller can look forward to a top-class introduction to one of the world's most underrated cuisines.

Russians love good food

Eating Habits

Most Russians are less concerned with *what* they eat than with getting enough of it. Many are struggling to maintain any eating habit at all. Consequently, tourists should bear in mind that they are in a somewhat artificial position. Although Caspian caviar and Siberian salmon are indeed key elements of the traditional menu, most citizens get by on large quantities of bread, potatoes and cabbage.

The Russian breakfast is generally a light affair centred on a good deal of strong, black tea, cold meat and cheese. It is often accompanied by *kefir*, a yoghurt-like drink much praised for its stomach-settling qualities the morning after the night before. Hotel breakfasts may add extra delicacies such as *blini* (pancakes) with honey.

Soups are very much a lunchtime dish, served piping hot and with a generous spoonful of soured cream stirred in. *Pirozhki* (savoury doughnuts), a variation on ravioli called *pelmyeni* and the southern favourite of *shashlyk* – meat kebabs – are also midday staples, often served up with boiled buckwheat or a mayonnaise-doused salad. A slice of black bread, as with any meal, is always on offer.

Blini with black caviar – a meal for kings

Dinner is easily the most elaborate meal and, if eating out, Russians like to make an occasion of it. Hot and cold *zakuski* (hors d'oeuvre) – typically smoked fish, wild mushrooms, hams and *blini* with red or black caviar – are almost enough in themselves, but Russians spread the load with dancing, philosophical debate and loquacious toasting throughout the evening. Traditionally, there is little concept of a quiet night out for two!

Drinking

Deeply ingrained in the culture despite occasional efforts to eradicate it, drinking on a grand scale is a national tradition and is focused firmly on the vodka bottle. Vodka (*see pp170–1*) is drunk neat in shots, preferably chilled, and followed up with a bite of marinaded fish or pickled cucumber. Be warned – Russian tolerance of vodka is famously higher than that of most tourists. One or two toasts are unavoidable, but then exercise a little caution, remembering that vodka-induced drunkenness steals up extremely rapidly.

The other great Russian love is tea. Drunk in copious quantities and without milk, tea is often served with a side saucer of homemade jam in place of sugar. Coffee is also highly prized, usually presented Turkish-style and heavily sweetened unless you specify otherwise (*byez sakhara* – without sugar).

Table etiquette

A meal out in Russia involves a greater emphasis on etiquette than in the West, with men expected to seat their partners and administer all drinks. (Single women should never be seated at the table corner – as any *babushka* will tell you, this means they will not marry for seven years!)

It is bad luck to leave empty bottles on the table, bad form not to finish opened ones, and a round of drinks should always be preceded by a toast. Toasts to health (*vashye zdorovye!*) require you to down your glassful in one. Smoking is acceptable at all junctures of the evening and non-smoking areas in restaurants are rare indeed.

If invited back home to eat, you ought to bring along a contribution to the meal (chocolates or a bottle of something) and flowers for your hostess.

Summer gardens appear throughout the city with the first rays of summer sun

MENU GUIDE (stressed syllables in *italics*)

Meals
ЗАВТРАК – *zah*vtrak – **breakfast**
ОБЕД – ab*yed* – **lunch**
УЖИН – *oo*zhin – **dinner**
ЗАКУСКИ – za*koo*ski – **starters/
appetisers**
САЛАТ – sa*laht* – **salad**
СУП – *soop* – **soup**
ПЕРВЫЕ БЛЮДА – p*yer*viye b*lyoo*da –
first course, usually soup
ВТОРЫЕ БЛЮДА – vto*ree*ye b*lyoo*da
– **second or 'hot' course**
ДЕСЕРТ – de*syert* – **dessert**
ФРУКТЫ – *frook*ti – **fruit**

Meat and Fish
МЯСО – *myas*a – **meat**
ГОВЯДИНА – gav*yahd*ina – **beef**
СВИНИНА – svi*neen*a – **pork**
БАРАНИНА – ba*rahn*ina –
lamb/mutton
ТЕЛЯТИНА – tel*yaht*ina – **veal**
КУРИЦА – *koor*itsa – **chicken**
КОЛБАСА – kolba*sah* – **sausage**
РЫБА – *ri*ba – **fish**
ЛОСОСЬ / ГОРБУША / СЁМГА –
la*sos*/gar*boo*sha/*syom*ga – **salmon**
ТРЕСКА – tres*ka* – **cod**
ФОРЕЛЬ – far*yel* – **trout**
ОСЕТРИНА / СЕВРЮГА – asye*treen*a /
se*vryoo*ga – **sturgeon**
ЧЁРНАЯ / КРАСНАЯ ИКРА –
*chyor*naya/ *kras*naya i*krah* –
black/red caviar

Vegetables, Fruit and Other Foods
МОРКОВЬ – mar*kohv* – **carrots**
СВЁКЛА – *svyok*la – **beetroot**
КАПУСТА – ka*poos*ta – **cabbage**
КАРТОФЕЛЬ – kar*tofe*l – **potatoes**
ЛУК – *look* – **onion**
ОГУРЦЫ – agoort*si* – **cucumber**

ПОМИДОЫ – pomi*dori* – **tomatoes**
ЯБЛОКО – *yah*bloka – **apple**
АПЕЛЬСИН – apel*seen* – **orange**
ДЫНЯ – *deen*ya – **melon**
БАНАН – ba*nahn* – **banana**
ЯЙЦА – *yait*sa – **eggs**
РИС – *rees* – **rice**
ХЛЕВ – *khlyeb* – **bread**
МОРОЖЕНОЕ – mar*ozh*enoye –
ice cream
ТОРТ – *tort* – **cake, gâteau**

Cooking Methods
КОПЧЁННЫЙ – kap*chyon*y – **smoked**
ВАРЁННЫЙ – var*yon*y – **boiled**
ЖАРЕННЫЙ – *zhar*eny – **fried**
ПЕЧЁННЫЙ – pe*chyon*y – **baked**
СОЛЁННЫЙ – sal*yon*y – **salted**

Traditional Dishes
ВИНЕГРЕТ – vinye*gryet* – **diced
vegetable salad**
САЛАТ ОЛИВЬЕ / СТОЛИЧНЫЙ
САЛАТ – sal*aht* oliv*yeh*, stol*eech*ny
sal*aht* – **diced meat, potatoes and
vegetables in mayonnaise or soured
cream**
БОРЩ – *borshch* – **beetroot soup**
ЩИ – *shchi* – **cabbage soup**
УХА – oo*kha* – **fish soup**
СОЛЯНКА – sal*yahn*ka – **thick fish or
meat soup with potatoes**
ОКРОШКА – a*krosh*ka – **cold soup
made from salad, cold meat
and kvas**
ГРИБЫ – gri*bi* – **mushrooms, often
marinaded or baked in soured
cream**
БЛИНЫ – bli*ni* – **small pancakes,
traditionally served with soured
cream and caviar**

ПЕЛЬМЕНИ – pel*myen*i – **a heavy version of ravioli served in soured cream**

ПИРОЖКИ – pirazh*ki* – **pies of meat, cabbage, etc in fried dough**

БЕФСТРОГАНОВ – byef*stroh*ganov – **beef stroganoff, strips of beef in sour cream sauce**

КОТЛЕТЫ ПО КИЕВСКИЙ – kaht*lyeh*ti pa *kee*yevsky – **chicken Kiev**

КУЛИБЯКА – kooli*byah*ka – **generally fish, especially salmon, en croûte**

ГОЛУБЦЫ – golubt*si* – **cabbage leaves stuffed with meat and rice**

ЖАРКОЕ – *zhar*koye – **spicy meat casserole in earthenware pot**

ШАШЛЫК – shash*leek* – **kebabed meat**

ХАЧАПУРИ – khacha*poor*i – **Caucasian flat bread stuffed with cheese**

Sauces and Condiments

СМЕТАНА – sme*tahn*a – **soured cream**

МАЙОНЕЗ – maiyon*ehz* – **mayonnaise**

ТОМАТНЫЙ СОУС – to*maht*ny sohs – **tomato sauce**

СЛИВОЧНОЕ МАСЛО – *sleev*ochnoye *mah*sla – **butter**

СОЛЬ – *sohl* – **salt**

ПЕРЕЦ – py*er*ets – **pepper**

ГОРЧИЦА – gar*cheet*sa – **mustard**

САХАР – *sakh*ar – **sugar**

Drinks

ВОДА – va*dah* – **water**

МИНЕРАЛЬНАЯ ВОДА (С ГАЗОМ/ БЕЗ ГАЗА)– miner*ahl*naya va*dah* (*sgahz*om/byez *gahz*a) – **mineral water (carbonated/still)**

СОК – sok – **fruit juice**

БЕЛОЕ / КРАСНОЕ ВИНО – byel*oye*/ *kras*noye vi*noh* – **white/red wine**

СЛАДКОЕ / СУХОЕ – slad*koye*/ su*khoye* – **sweet/dry**

ВОДКА – *vod*ka – **vodka**

КОНЬЯК – kon*yahk* – **brandy**

ПИВО – *pee*va – **beer**

ШАМПАНСКОЕ – sham*pahn*skoye – **'champagne' (Russian sparkling wine)**

ЛИКЁРЫ – lik*yor*i – **liqueurs**

ЧАЙ (С МОЛОКОМ / С ЛИМОНОМ / С САХАРОМ / БЕЗ САХАРА) – chai (smal*akom* / sli*moh*nom / *sakh*arom / byez *sakh*ara) – **tea (with milk, lemon, sugar, without sugar)**

КОФЕ (С САХАРОМ / БЕЗ САХАРА) – *koh*fye (*sakh*arom / byez *sakh*ara) – **coffee (with/without sugar)**

Useful Words and Phrases

РЕСТОРАН – ryesta*rahn* – **restaurant**

КАФЕ – ka*feh* – **café**

БАР – *bar* – **bar**

МЕНЮ – men*yoo* – **menu**

ОФИЦИАНТ – afits*yant* – **waiter**

СТАКАН – sta*kahn* – **glass (tumbler)**

БОКАЛ – ba*kahl* – **glass (wine glass)**

ЧАШКА – *chash*ka – **cup**

ТАРЕЛКА – tar*yel*ka – **plate**

НОЖ – *nozh* – **knife**

ВИЛКА – *veel*ka – **fork**

ЛОЖКА – *lozh*ka – **spoon**

ТУАЛЕТ – tooah*lyet* – **washroom**

ПЕПЕЛЬНИЦА – py*e*pelneetsa – **ashtray**

МОЖНО ЕЩЁ…? – *mozh*ma yesh*yoh* …? – **May I have some more …?**

ЭТО НЕСЪЕДОБНО – *eh*ta nyesye*dob*na – **This is inedible**

МОЖНО СЧЁТ, ПОЖАЛУИСТА? – *mozh*na shyot, pazhal*sta*? – **May I have the bill, please?**

СДАЧИ НЕ НАДО – *sdach*i nye *na*da – **Keep the change**

НА ЧАЙ – na *chai* – **tip**

RESTAURANTS, BARS AND CAFÉS

The choice of good eating and drinking establishments in both cities is rapidly expanding, though quality and price level seesaw dramatically. These listings concentrate on the tried and trusted.

A Few Tips

An increasing number of restaurants accept credit cards, but it is wise to come well supplied with roubles. Very few now take foreign currency in cash even if the menu prices are quoted in dollars.

Vegetarians are poorly catered for in general. (If necessary, ask the waiter for help: *Ya nye yem myaso* – I don't eat meat; *Kakiye oo vas blyooda byez myasa?* – What dishes do you have without meat?)

Always book in advance (ask your hotel to do this). In winter, take a change of footwear to the restaurant rather than suffer wet boots all evening.

Tip as you would in Europe (10 to 15 per cent). The cloakroom attendant will also expect a small gratuity.

Price Guide

Poorer Russians seldom eat out, so many restaurants are in the medium-to-expensive bracket. As a rough guide, reckon on the following categories per head without alcohol:

* less than $15 rouble equivalent (less than £9)
** from $15 to $25 (from £9–£15)
*** $25 to $50 (from £15–£30)
**** over $50 (over £30)

Beer costs between $3 and $8 per 500ml; vodka costs $3 to $7 per domestic bottle, twice that for imported. Wine and champagne vary considerably, locally-produced brands being greatly cheaper.

MOSCOW

RESTAURANTS

1 Krasnaya Ploshchad ***

The name (Number 1 Red Square) says it all. This recently refurbished restaurant, in the Historical Museum, serves up tasty imperial-era cuisine. *Krasnaya Ploshchad 1. Tel: 925 3600. www.redsquare.ru. Open: noon–midnight. Metro: Ploshchad Revolyutsii/Okhotniy Ryad.*

American Bar & Grill */**

Saloon-style American restaurant. *1-ya Tverskaya-Yamskaya 2. Tel: 250 9525. Open: non-stop. Metro: Mayakovskaya. Zemlyanoy Val 59. Tel: 912 3615, 912 3621. Open: daily noon–2am. Metro: Taganskaya. Vorontsovskaya 50. Tel: 276 4096. Open: daily noon–2am. Metro: Proletarskaya.*

Aristokrat */**

Coffee house in wing of a 19th-century house. Great coffees, teas and cakes. *Myasnitskaya 37. Tel: 924 0702. Open: daily 10am–midnight. Metro: Chistiye Prudy.*

Baan Thai ***

Authentic and reliable Thai favourites.

Russia offers a range of stylish restaurants in romantic settings, but at a price

Bolshaya Dorogomilovskaya 11. Tel: 240 0597. Open: noon–midnight. www.baanthai.ru. Metro: Kievskaya.

Botchka ***

A pleasant setting for local and international food. *Ulitsa 1905 goda 2. Tel: 252 3041. www.botchka.ru. Open: non-stop. Metro: Ulitsa 1905 goda.*

Bulvar ****

French and fusion food; collar and tie and reservations essential. *Petrovka 30/7. Tel: 209 6798. Open: noon–midnight. Metro: Chekhovskaya.*

Carre Blanc ****

Haute cuisine in French-owned restaurant. *Seleznevskaya 19/2. Tel: 258 4403. www.carreblanc.ru. Open: daily noon–midnight. Metro: Novoslobodskaya.*

Da Cicco */**

This *trattoria* is great if you are after pizza and pasta. *Profsoyuznaya 13/12. Tel: 125 1196. www.da-cicco.menu.ru. Open: noon–11pm. Metro: Profsoyuznaya.*

Duboviy zal TsDL ****

Excellent restaurant in the former House of Writers with great Russian cuisine. Great atmosphere. *Povarskaya 50.*

Tel: 291 1515. Open: noon–midnight. Metro: Barrikadnaya.

Grin ***

Mediterranean dishes prepared by Spanish chef. *Kutuzovskiy Prospekt 12. Tel: 243 6407. Open: daily noon–midnight. Metro: Kievskaya.*

Gostinaya */**

Coffee house with good choice of coffees, teas and cocktails. Summer terrace. *Shmitovskiy Proyezd 3. Tel: 256 0881. Open: 1pm–2am Mon–Wed, Sun, 1pm–3am Thur–Sat. Metro: Ulitsa 1905 goda.*

Mama Zoya **

Popular Georgian restaurant on a boat. *Fruzenskaya Naberezhnaya 16b. Tel: 242 8550. Open: daily noon–11pm. No credit cards. Metro: Frunzenskaya.*

Moscow–Bombay **

Indian restaurant. *Glinishchevskiy Pereulok 3. Tel: 292 9375. Open: daily 11am–11pm. Metro: Pushkinskaya.*

Noev Kovcheg **/***

Fine Armenian food. *Maliy Ivanovskiy Pereulok 9. Tel: 917 0717. www.noevkovcheg.ru. Open: noon–midnight. Metro: Kitay-Gorod.*

Nostalzhi ***/****

Quiet French restaurant.

Tchistoprudniy Bulvar 12a. Tel: 925 7625. Open: daily noon–midnight. Metro: Tchistiye Prudy.

Pancho Villa **/***

Good Mexican food, including steaks. Now moved to *Bolshaya Yakimanka 52. Tel: 238 7913. Metro: Oktyabrskaya.*

Pushkin **/***

Prize-winning café and restaurant, Russian cuisine. *Tverskoy Bulvar 26a. Tel: 229 5590. Open: daily noon–midnight. Metro: Pushkinskaya.*

Settebello **/***

Stylish Italian restaurant. *Sadovaya-Samotechnaya 3. Tel: 299 3039. Open: daily noon–midnight. Metro: Tsvetnoy Bulvar.*

Shinok ***

Ukrainian restaurant offering their typical foods. *Ulitsa 1905 goda 2. Tel: 255 0204. www.shinik.ru. Open: non-stop. Metro: Ulitsa 1905 goda.*

Temple Bar */**

Convenient stopover for shoppers, this large English-style pub-restaurant serves a range of hearty fare and beers. *Manezh Shopping Mall (Aleksandrovskiy Sad entrance). Tel: 737 8476. Open 24 hours daily. Metro: Okhotniy Ryad.*

The Real Mccoy **
Pop into this 'speakeasy' in one of the Stalin skyscrapers to enjoy a snack, steak or cocktail. *Kudrinskaya Ploshchad. Tel: 255 4144. www.mccoy.ru. Open 24 hours daily. Metro: Barrikadnaya.*

Uzbekistan ****
Uzbek, Arabic and Chinese cuisine. *Neglinnaya 29/14. Tel: 923 0585. Open: daily noon–midnight. Metro: Teatralnaya.*

ST PETERSBURG RESTAURANTS

1913 **/****
Popular with well-heeled locals, this is a traditional Russian restaurant serving classic but uncomplicated fare. *Voznesenskiy Prospekt 13/2. Tel: 315 5148. Open: noon–1am. Metro: Nevskiy Prospekt or Sadovaya.*

Da Vinci ***
Five different cuisines and a great variety of wines in this restaurant-bar with live music. *Ul Malaya Morskaya 15. Tel: 311 0173. Open: noon–6am. Metro: Nevskiy Prospekt.*

Idiot ***
One of the best vegetarian restaurants in the city. *Nab reki Moyki 82. Tel:*

315 1675. Metro: Sadovaya.

Kalinka-Malinka **
The best of national cuisine. Great variety of folk entertainment. *Italianskaya ul 5. Tel: 314 2681. www.kalinka-malinka. spb.ru. Metro: Nevskiy Prospekt.*

Karavan-saray **
Colourful Uzbek restaurant with tasty regional dishes; also belly dancing shows. *Nekrasova 1. Tel: 273 4205. www.caravan-saray.ru. Open: noon till late. Metro: Mayakovskaya, then trolley bus 3 or 8.*

Kavkaz Bar ***
Live music, more than 70 excellent Georgian wines. *Karavannaya ul 18. Tel: 312 1665. www.kavkazbar.ru. Open: (café) 11am–8pm, (restaurant) 11am–1am. Metro: Gostiniy Dvor/Nevskiy Prospekt.*

Landskrona ****
Petersburg's best. Top-class dining and roof-top patio. *Nevskiy Palace Hotel, Nevskiy Pr 57. Tel: 380 2001. Open: 6.30pm–midnight. Metro: Mayakovskaya.*

Le Français ****
More than 60 traditional French dishes and a big choice of French wines.

Galernaya ul 20. Tel: 315 2465. www.lefrancais.spb.ru. Open: 11am–1am. Metro: Sadovaya.

Literaturnoe Café **/***
Pushkin's favourite. Overrated but attractive. *Nevskiy Prospekt 18. Tel: 312 6057. www.labrint.ru/ restoran/lit-cafe. Metro: Nevskiy Prospekt.*

New Island ***
European cuisine. Ship restaurant that is often visited by the presidents. *Rumyantsevskiy spusk. Tel: 963 6765. Open: 11am–11pm. Metro: Vasileostrovskaya.*

Pirosmani **
Cosy Georgian restaurant with old Tbilisi interiors. *Bolshoy Prospekt 14. Tel: 235 6456. www.pirosmani.spb.ru. Metro: Sportivnaya.*

Taleon ****
Exclusive French restaurant in the former mansion of the merchant Yeliseev. *Nab. Reki Moyki 59. Tel: 312 5373. www.taleon.ru. Open 7pm–3am. Booking (and formal dress) essential. Metro: Nevskiy Prospekt.*

Tbilisi *
Reasonable Georgian outfit. Small but popular. Live music. *Sytninskaya Ulitsa 10. Tel: 232 9391.*

Open: noon–11.30pm.
Metro: Gorkovskaya.

MOSCOW BARS AND CAFÉS

Bars

Bavarius
Beer house serves large selection of local and imported beer, and meals ideally suited to them.
Komsomolskiy Prospekt 21/10. Tel: 247 4155. www.bavarius.ru. Open: daily noon–midnight. Metro: Frunzenskaya. Sadovaya-Triumfalnaya 2/30. Tel: 299 4211. Open: daily noon–midnight. Metro: Mayakovskaya.

BB King's
Posters of jazz and blues greats, appropriate live music, bar food.
Sadovaya-Samotechnaya Ulitsa 4. Tel: 299 8206. Metro: Tsvetnoy Bulvar.

Rosie O'Grady's
Very convincing imitation of a pub with draught Guinness, Sky Sport and Sunday lunches.
Znamenka 9/12. Tel: 502 0752. www.rosie.ru. Open: noon–late. Metro: Borovitskaya.

Cafés

Bookafe
Refreshingly low-key, modish café with photography and art books to hand while enjoying a cappuccino or glass of wine.
Sadovaya-Samotochnaya 13. Tel: 200 0356. Open 11am–2am. Metro: Tsvetnoy Bulvar.

Coffee Bean
Two cafés in the city with excellent coffee and cakes.
Pokrovka 18. Tel: 923 9793. Open: 8am–10pm Mon–Thur, 8am–11pm Fri–Sat, 9am–10pm Sun. Metro: Kitay Gorod. Tverskaya 10. Tel: 788 6357. Open: 8am–11pm Mon–Sat, 9am–11pm Sun. Metro: Pushkinskaya.

Délifrance
Croissant and cappuccino to die for, but at a price.
Tverskaya 31 (enter through the lobby of the concert hall). Tel: 299 4284. Open: 9am–11.30pm. Metro: Mayakovskaya.

Hard Rock Café
The Moscow branch of the famous café chain, the second largest in Europe, occupies a classy stucco building in the Arbat.
Stary Arbat 44. Tel: 244 8970. Open: 24 hours daily. Metro: Arbatskaya.

ST PETERSBURG BARS AND CAFÉS

Bars

The Caviar Bar
Stunning Art-Nouveau setting in the Grand Hotel Europe.
Mikhailovskaya ul 1/7. Tel: 329 6000. www.grand-hotel-Europe.com/web/ stpetersburg. Metro: Gostiniy Dvor.

Chaika
German bar with wurst and sauerkraut.
Kanal Griboyedova Naberezhnaya 14. Tel: 312 4631. www.chaika.ru. Metro: Nevskiy Prospekt.

Mollie's Irish Bar
Good pub food and welcoming atmosphere. The city's best bar.
Rubinshteyna 36. Tel: 319 9768. Open: noon–5am. Metro: Vladimirskaya/ Mayakovskaya.

Cafés

Idealnaya Chashka
A chain of coffee and confectionery cafés.
Nevskiy Pr 15, 112, 130. www.idealcup.ru

Laima Bistro
Excellent Russian bistro chain, serving snacks and light meals. No smoking or credit cards.
Nab Kanala Griboyedova 14–16. Tel: 318 9219. Open 24 hours daily. Metro: Nevskiy Prospekt or Gostiniy Dvor. Bolshoy Prospekt 88. Metro: Petrogradskaya.

V o d k a

'Drinking is the joy of Russians,' declared Prince Vladimir in 988. A millennium later, Russians are still hard at it, consuming more alcohol than any other Europeans – on average nearly three times as much as the British.

The national drink is vodka, meaning 'little water', reputedly invented by Russian monks in the 14th century. Produced from filtered water and pure spirit, it is drunk neat, chilled and in one gulp, traditionally followed by a bite of pickled cucumber or a deep sniff from a chunk of black bread – said to help it go down more smoothly.

The ingredients of the commercially manufactured article vary slightly: *Stolichnaya* includes a little sugar syrup, *Moskovskaya* has a drop or two of vinegar added and *Pshenichnaya* is made from distilled potatoes. Other brands are infused with lemon oil, peppers or bison grass.

By contrast, *samogon* – moonshine – is made from whatever comes to hand. Rye, wheat, sugar and potatoes are the ingredients of choice, but Russians are adept at

creating homebrew from toothpaste, boot polish – even cockroach powder. Journalists reporting the war in Chechnya were plagued with Russian requests for colour photographic film, a key ingredient of an especially lethal infusion.

Peter the Great's troops received two mugfuls daily by imperial decree. Peter established the state monopoly on vodka production, and used the proceeds to help finance his wars. Vodka played her role in the Great Patriotic War of 1941–5. On 22 August 1941, Joseph Stalin issued a decree no. 56200 which secured the so-called 'Commissars 100 grams' of vodka which were issued daily to all soldiers fighting on the frontline. Today, vodka revenues rake in more than income tax: one million bottles a day are sold in Moscow alone.

A secret report, commissioned by the government in 1980, concluded that drinking had become a threat to national security. It spurred Gorbachev to cut vodka production drastically in the hope of forcing the population back to the workplace. But the policy succeeded only in driving production underground and emptying shops of sugar, potatoes and eau de Cologne, while employees spent ever longer queueing for the few bottles that remained on sale – then drank their contents.

In June 2003, the Russian Government took measures to prevent the misuse of the label 'Russian Vodka'. A patent was issued by which a product carrying the 'Russian Vodka' label must be distilled and bottled solely in Russia and must pass a taste test.

Russian vodka is drunk in 'grams', preferably one hundred grams at any one time. One hundred grams equals 100ml of this potent fluid. Foreign visitors who do not feel confident in drinking such a large quantity are often tolerated and will only be expected to drink 50 grams! Sipping vodka, or mixing it with juice or any other alcohol-free beverage, should be avoided at all costs as it is perceived to be something quite strange. Protocol allows you to 'wash down' vodka with another beverage after drinking it straight.

Russians do not accept any excuses for not having a 'stakan' (glass/shot of vodka) with them. If visitors try to excuse themselves, their hosts usually take it as a joke and pour them a glass anyway! Once the vodka is poured there is no escape. Excuses that tend to work include blaming your sobriety on the need to drive home (make sure you have a car in Moscow), diabetes, and women are excused by pregnancy, but their partners will be expected to drink even more to celebrate this joyous occasion.

In Russia vodka is used as a medicament. It can be rubbed into your sore limbs to ease the pain or mixed with black pepper to ease colds and flu (temperatures are lowered by rubbing vodka into your entire body). Needless to say, it can also be used to rinse your teeth with when they hurt.

Try visiting the Vodka Museum in St Petersburg, open daily from 11am to 10pm. It can be located at 5, Konnogvardeisky bv., St Petersburg. Tel: 812 312 9178; fax: 812 312 3416. www.vodkamuseum.ru/english/museum

Vodka, the national drink and a source of joy as well as problems for most Russians

Hotels and Accommodation

In the days when tourism was a state monopoly, the foreign traveller was lucky to know in which hotel he was to be housed before arrival at the airport. Happily, the situation has changed for the better. Although Russia's hotel industry still has some catching up to do, you can now enjoy first-class standards of accommodation – if you can afford it.

You can stay in stylish old hotels dating back to the pre-communist era …

The adventurous might consider staying with a Russian family for an unrivalled insider's view of what life is really like (*see p175*).

The First Step

Choose and book accommodation with your travel agent before arrival.

Alternatively, shop around on the Internet or contact one of the growing number of accommodation agencies in both cities (*see p189 for a selection of agents*).

Good-quality, Western-style hotels are relatively few in number and often heavily booked. Their ex-Soviet

… or you can check in to a communist mega-project such as Hotel Russia

counterparts are frequently all but empty, yet the barrage of paperwork, calls to the police and hostile reception staff that greet unexpected arrivals are a serious disincentive to fully independent travel. At the very least, book your St Petersburg accommodation while you are in Moscow (and vice versa).

(*See p175 for bed and breakfast booking.*)

Selecting a Hotel
Neither Moscow nor St Petersburg has the huge number of affordable hotels and guest houses that characterise, say, London or Paris. This simplifies your choice.

Western-run hotels are four or five star, mostly operated by chains such as Radisson or Marco Polo, and are all one would expect from an international luxury hotel, the tariff included. Expect to pay between £140 and £200 for a double room.

Former Soviet establishments are notably cheaper (the better ones cost about £70 for a double, the less pleasant as little as £15), but are generally spartan, unloved and under-maintained. Their own star grading system is a deceptive guide to the quality within. Broken televisions, eccentric plumbing, drunken trade union delegations and vermin are not considered grounds for a discount. Four stars is the top of the range and the least likely to offer the above inconveniences. However, it is vital to check in advance when the establishment was last refurbished.

Location
Most Western-style hotels are situated in the centre of both cities. Those which

are not offer a regular shuttle service to and from the centre. Location is more critical with regard to Soviet-style hotels, many of which are in industrialised suburbs: the savings may not be worth the trouble of commuting into town each day. Check the location carefully before booking.

Having chosen the hotel, ask for a room that does not face the street. Russian traffic runs on low-grade petrol – the smell can be overpowering – and at night you run the risk of being kept awake by the noise.

Understanding your Hotel
There should be no difficulties with a Western-style hotel. You will find most staff speak English. Restaurants, gymnasiums and souvenir shops are liberally distributed about the premises. Breakfast is usually included in the room price (you generally have the choice from an extensive buffet) and credit cards are accepted. Most will also offer facilities for changing money and many are equipped with state-of-the-art business centres.

Soviet-style establishments, however, work according to their own subculture, which takes some adjusting to. With your key you will be issued a pass essential to getting past the doorman later. Always lock your door and do not open it to unknown visitors under any circumstances. The key should be left with the lady manning your floor, the *dezhurnaya*, who can also serve you tea or at least hot water.

The hotel's restaurants and bars may keep illogical hours – it is worth

Hotel Ukraine presents you with an opportunity to stay in one of Stalin's skyscrapers

Hostels

A good option for the budget-conscious is the traveller's hostel, aimed at Western backpackers but clean and secure and an excellent source of camaraderie and local knowledge. Accommodation is generally in dormitories, though some two-bed rooms are available. A communal breakfast is offered in the morning and self-catering facilities are available for general use.

There is one well-known hostel in each of the two cities and booking ahead of a planned trip is essential to avoid disappointment, especially during high points of the season such as the St Petersburg White Nights. Both are under foreign management and the staff speak English. They can also help arrange visa invitations (*see p178*) and organise travel tickets within Russia – between Moscow and St Petersburg or something as exotic as the Trans-Siberian Railway.

checking to avoid disappointment later. Breakfast is rarely included in the room price and credit cards are almost never acceptable.

Checking out can be a time-consuming process since the *dezhurnaya* will want to inspect your rooms to ensure towels etc are all intact. Give yourself ample time if you have a plane or train to catch!

In Moscow try the **Moscow Travelers Guest House**, *Bolshaya Pereslavskaya 50, 10th floor. Tel: (095) 631 4059; fax: (095) 280 7686. www.tgh.ru. Metro: Prospekt Mira.*

In St Petersburg try the **St Petersburg International Hostel**, *3-ya Sovetskaya 28. Tel: 329 8018; fax: 329 8019. www.ryh.ru. Metro: Ploshchad Vosstaniya.*

Self-catering

Self-catering accommodation in furnished apartments is not a feasible short-term option, but those who are planning to stay for a month or more should check the English-language press classified sections for rental advertisements. Most flats are very basic by Western standards of comfort. Those with modern electrical appliances and a fresh coat of paint are likely to be as expensive as rented accommodation in any other major capital. However, it works out much cheaper than a hotel.

For camping possibilities, *see p179.*

Bed and breakfast

Living with a Russian family is the ideal way to become acquainted with

Youth hostels come in handy if you have a limited budget

The lavish interior of the ground-floor restaurant in The Metropol Hotel, Moscow

life beyond the holiday brochures and tour buses. It is also surprisingly well organised in both cities and can be pre-booked prior to arrival.

Prices per night vary but range from about £15 to £20 for rooms checked by agency staff and for a mammoth Russian breakfast. Most of the hosts either speak fluent English or are students keen to improve their grasp of the language. Some may be happy to work as a driver for the duration of your stay or might offer their services as a guide to the city.

For Moscow and St Petersburg, contact **Home Families Association**, *www.hofa.ru*

On Business

Economic reforms in the former Soviet Union opened the floodgates of investment opportunities for foreign business. The rapidly developing market has given Moscow and St Petersburg a frontier atmosphere of enterprise, leading observers to refer ironically to the new 'Wild East'.

Detail of a building bearing the coat of arms of the USSR

HOTEL BUSINESS CENTRES

Most Western-style hotels have business centres, and both cities can provide communications, translation/interpretation and printing services.

Moscow:

Business Centre, Hotel Metropol
Teatralniy Proezd 1/4. Tel: 927 6090. www.metropol-moscow.ru. Metro: Teatralnaya.

Radisson Slavyanskaya Hotel
Berezhkovskaya Naberezhnaya 2. Tel: 941 8427. www.radissonmoscow.ru

St Petersburg:

Grand Hotel Europe Business Centre
Mikhaylovskaya Ulitsa 1/7. Tel: 329 6670/73.

Hotel Neptun Business Centre
Obvodnovo Kanal Naberezhnaya 93a. Tel: 324 4600. www.neptun.spb.ru

Kareliya Hotel Business Centre
Ul Tuhachevskoyo 27/2. Tel: 718 4004. www.karelia.spb.ru

OTHER BUSINESS CENTRES

In Moscow:

Millennium House
Trubnaya 12. Tel: 787 2757/2751; fax: 787 2767. www.millenniumhouse.ru

Russian Federation Chamber of Commerce, Department of Foreign Relations
Ilynka 6. Tel: 929 0334; fax: 929 0355.

ZAO Expocentre
Krasnaya Presnya Exhibition Complex, 1st Krasnogvardeyskiy Proyezd 12.

In St Petersburg:

Business Communication Centre
Bolshaya Morskaya 3/5. Tel: 314 0140; fax: 314 3360. Metro: Nevskiy Prospekt/Gostiniy Dvor.

Chamber of Commerce and Industry
Chaikovskova 46–48. Tel: 119 6644/275 0988; fax: 272 6406. www.spbcci.ru/eng.

SPIBA (St Petersburg International Business Association)
Shpalernaya 36. Tel: 325 9091; fax: 279 9789. www.spiba.spb.ru

Business Travel

American Express Travel Services
are based in Moscow at: *Usachova 33, bldg 1. Tel: 933 6633/8447.*
In St Petersburg: *Malaya Morskaya 23. Tel: 326 4500.*
www.americanexpress.ru

Commercial Sections

The commercial section of your embassy in Moscow may be able to help with current trading information and put you in touch with partners and colleagues.

UK: *Smolenskaya nab.10.*
Tel: 956 7477/956 7200.
www.britemb.msk.ru
USA: *Novinskiy Bulvar 19.*
Tel: 728 5000/5577.
www.usembassy.state.gov
Ireland: *Grokholskiy Pereulok 5.*
Tel: 937 5900/11.

Communications
Better hotels offer satellite links for calls.
Fax modems are now capable of
international communications. Some
business centres can arrange temporary
e-mail accounts. Another option for
AT&T calling card holders is available
in Moscow – to be connected, call *155
5042* and quote your number. If you
are not a card holder, you can still
use the service to make collect calls
to the USA.

Finally, a series of satellite telephones
in Moscow is operated by Comstar
communications. Call *250 2131* for
details of the closest. In St Petersburg,
several international pay phones have
been installed in the city centre.
Instructions are provided in several
different languages and credit cards are
on sale widely.

CONFERENCE CENTRES AND EXHIBITION HALLS
Most Western-style hotels offer
conference facilities. Listed below are the
main trade exhibition sites. For advice
on putting on your own show, consult
the business centres (*see opposite*) or
contact the following institutions:
Moscow:
All-Russia Exhibition Centre
(VVTs/VDNKh)

Selskokhozyaystvennaya. Tel: 974 5366.
Metro: Prospekt Mira.
**International Trade Centre Exhibition
Complex**
Krasnopresnenskaya Naberezhnaya 12–14.
*Exhibitions tel: 255 3799. Congress Centre
tel: 253 1140/253 8117.*
St Petersburg:
Central Exhibition Hall Manege
Isaakievskaya Pl 1. Tel: 314 8248;
fax: 314 8254.
LenEXPO Travel Company
Bolshoy Prospekt 103. Tel: 321 2610; fax:
321 2652. www.lenexpotravel.ru/eng
SKK Exhibition Complex
Prospekt Yuriy gagarina 8. Tel: 298 1211.

Consultancy
Many major Western accountants/
consultants are already well established:
PriceWaterhouseCoopers
Kosmodamyanskaya Naberezhnaya 52.
Tel: 967 6000. Sredniy Prospekt 36/40,
St Petersburg. Tel: 326 6969.
www.pwcglobal.com

Graphics and Printing
Printing, photocopying and design
services are offered in Moscow by
AlphaGraphics, *Nikoloyamskaya 14.*
Tel: 730 5557. www.alphagraphics.ru

A subway station can also be beautiful

P r a c t i c a l   G u i d e

Arriving
Visas and Registration
All visitors to Russia need a valid
passport with at least one blank page
and six months before the expiry date.
Visas (obligatory) are obtainable from
Russian embassies or consulates. A fee is
payable and the process is bureaucratic
and time-consuming. Package tourists
can expect their tour operator to
arrange the relevant Tourist Visa. To
qualify you need proof of pre-booked
accommodation for the relevant period.
Visitors staying in hostels or homestays
would be advised to contact a visa
agency in their home country well in
advance of travelling (*see below*).

Business visas, valid for three, six or
twelve months, can be obtained through
an official letter from an organisation in
Russia, accredited to the Ministry of
Foreign Affairs. Holders of business
visas do not need proof of pre-booked
accommodation. Visitors staying in large
hotels will automatically obtain the
obligatory Visa Registration stamp.
Those in hostels or homestays should
consult the host agency before
travelling. Without an exit stamp from
the Passport and Visa Directorate
(formerly known as OVIR) you will be
liable to a hefty fine.

For information on the latest visa
regulations and how to apply, contact
www.waytorussia.net/russianvisa

PVU (Moscow) *Pokrovka 42. Tel: 200
8487 (information tel: 208 2091). Open:
Mon, Tue, Thur, Fri 10am–2pm, 3–6pm
(metro: Kurskaya, Krasnie Vorota).* PVU

(St Petersburg) *Kirochnaya Ul 4. Tel: 278
3486. Open: Mon, Wed, Fri 10am–noon.*

The following travel agencies abroad
specialise in Russia and can arrange
visas:
UK:
Alpha-Omega Travel, *6 Beaconsfield
Court, Garforth, Leeds LS25 1QH
Tel: 0113 286 2121.*
Andrews Travel House London, *23
Pembridge Square, London W2 4DR.
Tel/fax: 020 7727 2838.*
USA:
Complete Travel & Visa Center,
*40 Rector Street, Suite 1504, New York,
NY 10006. Tel: 212 233 3332; fax: 212
233 0916. www.visatorussia.com*

By Air
Moscow has two international airports.
From **Domodedovo** take the shuttle
train to Paveletskiy vokzal (station) and
then metro (journey time 45 minutes).
Tickets are in roubles only. From
Sheremetevo-2 the cheapest option is
bus 851/minibus 48 to Rechnoy vokzal
or bus 817/minibus 49 to Planernaya
and then on by metro. A quicker, but far
more expensive (i.e. up to $100), option
is to take a taxi (journey time around
45 minutes depending on traffic). On no
account get into a taxi without agreeing
the fare first.

For flight information telephone:
(Domodedovo) *323 8160*;
(Sheremetevo-2) *956 4666.*

St Petersburg's international airport
is **Pulkovo 2**. For current information
on international flights, call *104 3444.*

The airport is 17km (11 miles) south of the city. Taxis are a slightly cheaper means of travelling in St Petersburg than in Moscow and the bus No. 13 route runs into the city, stopping at Moskovskaya Ploshchad (*Metro: Moskovskaya*).

By Rail

Those arriving in Moscow by train from Western Europe come into Belorusskiy Vokzal (Station), served by the metro's circle and green lines. Trains to St Petersburg from Helsinki pull into Finlandskiy Vokzal at Ploshchad Lenina metro, while those from Derbent and Berlin arrive at Vitebskiy Vokzal, Pushkinskaya metro station.

Camping

Moscow has two motels-cum-campsites. Neither is close to the centre of town and both are insecure.

Mozhayskiy, *Mozhayskoe Shosse 165. Tel: 447 4920. Open: June to mid-Sept.*

Butovo, *Butovo. Bolshaya Butovskaya 5. Tel: 712 7136. Open: June to mid-Sept.*

Of St Petersburg's two options (below), the first is preferable.

Retur-Motel, *Sestroretsk. Bolshaya Kupalnaya 28. Tel: 437 7533/434 5021.*

Olgino, *Primorskoe Shosse km 18. Tel: 336 3475/238 3043.*

Children

Children up to seven travel free on public transport. Aeroflot allows one child under five to travel with each accompanying adult on its internal flights. Most of the museums and parks offer discount tickets for children. Disposable nappies and baby foods are on sale in most Western-style supermarkets (*see p143*).

Climate

St Petersburg is slightly warmer than Moscow, but the damp and the Baltic breezes can make it seem colder. March

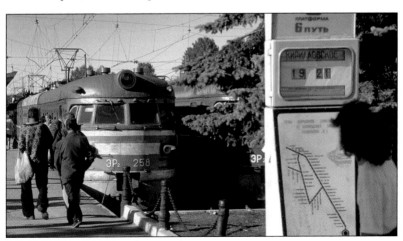

Finland Station, one of St Petersburg's rail termini

and early April bring slush and puddles during the thaw. Mid-May to mid-September sees temperatures averaging 18°C (64°F) in both cities, often reaching 25–30°C (77–86°F) in July and August. Winter draws in quickly by mid-October.

Moscow Weather Chart

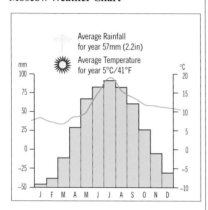

Average Rainfall for year 57mm (2.2in)

Average Temperature for year 5°C/41°F

St Petersburg Weather Chart

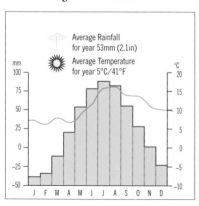

Average Rainfall for year 53mm (2.1in)

Average Temperature for year 5°C/41°F

WEATHER CONVERSION CHART
25.4mm = 1 inch
°F = 1.8 × °C + 32

Conversion Tables

Although Russia uses the same sizes as the rest of Europe for some items of clothing, other items can vary. (*See opposite.*)

Crime

The tourist is unlikely to encounter the much-reported organised criminal activity. Petty theft is comparable to that in major cities elsewhere. Do not leave valuables unattended, do not carry large amounts of cash, and always lock your hotel room. Be wary if a stranger invites you home. At night, be careful with taxi rides and keep to well-lit streets. Avoid the gangs of gypsy children in areas frequented by foreigners – they strip their victims of valuables like locusts. On overnight trains lock your compartment door and do not open it to strangers.

Customs

Russian customs regulations are many and ever-changing, but real problems only arise if you try to export tradable quantities of commodities like caviar, or antiques. This means steering clear of genuine icons and *objets d'art* (including books) produced more than 20 years ago. Items of military hardware and uniforms are also best avoided. Permits to export are available through the Office for Culture. *Tel: 921 3258.*

Fill in a currency declaration form on arrival, get receipts for each time you change money and fill in a form on departure. Roubles may not be exported.

Driving

Russian driving practices are hair-raising, and travelling by car in Moscow and St Petersburg is not recommended. Roads are potholed and badly signposted, and you are at the mercy of the GAI, the ill-reputed traffic police. Drivers must possess a home and international driving licence with Russian language insert (available from the AA). Russians often drive without insurance, so have a comprehensive policy (if driving a rented car, check the level and conditions of cover). It is illegal to drive after drinking any amount of alcohol.

Traffic drives on the right. The speed limit in built-up areas is 60kph and 80kph on highways. Petrol – *benzin* – comes in several octane grades, 95 being the best for Western cars. Unleaded is nonexistent.

Car hire agencies operating in Moscow and St Petersburg include:
Avis: Moscow, *tel: 684 1937.*
www.avis-moscow.ru
Biracs: *tel: 310 5356. www.biracs.ru*
Budget: *tel: 931 9700. www.budget.ru*
Europcar: International Reservations: *tel: 007095 783 7161. www.europcar.ru*
Hertz: Moscow, *tel: 937 3274.*
St Petersburg, *tel: 324 3242.*
www.hertz.spb.ru or *www.hertz.ru*

Electricity
Most of Russia runs on 220v and uses continental European-style 2-pin plugs. Many electrical stores and Western-style supermarkets sell adaptors.

EMBASSIES AND CONSULATES
Moscow (embassies):
Australia: *Kropotkinskiy Pereulok 13. Tel: 956 6070. www.australianembassy.ru*
Canada: *Starokonyushenniy Pereulok 23. Tel: 105 6000.*

Conversion Table

FROM	TO	MULTIPLY BY
Inches	Centimetres	2.54
Feet	Metres	0.3048
Yards	Metres	0.9144
Miles	Kilometres	1.6090
Acres	Hectares	0.4047
Gallons	Litres	4.5460
Ounces	Grams	28.35
Pounds	Grams	453.6
Pounds	Kilograms	0.4536
Tons	Tonnes	1.0160

To convert back, for example from centimetres to inches, divide by the number in the third column.

Men's Suits

UK	36	38	40	42	44	46	48
Russia/Rest of Europe	46	48	50	52	54	56	58
USA	36	38	40	42	44	46	48

Dress Sizes

UK	8	10	12	14	16	18
France	36	38	40	42	44	46
Italy	38	40	42	44	46	48
Russia	44	46	48	50	52	54
Rest of Europe	34	36	38	40	42	44
USA	6	8	10	12	14	16

Men's Shirts

UK	14	14.5	15	15.5	16	16.5	17
Russia/Rest of Europe	36	37	38	39/40	41	42	43
USA	14	14.5	15	15.5	16	16.5	17

Men's Shoes

UK	7	7.5	8.5	9.5	10.5	11
Russia	38	39	40	42	44	46
Rest of Europe	41	42	43	44	45	46
USA	8	8.5	9.5	10.5	11.5	12

Women's Shoes

UK	4.5	5	5.5	6	6.5	7
Russia/Rest of Europe	38	38	39	39	40	41
USA	6	6.5	7	7.5	8	8.5

Republic of Ireland: *Grokholskiy Pereulok 5. Tel: 937 5911.*
New Zealand: *Povarskaya 44. Tel: 956 3579. www.nzembassy.msk.ru*
UK: *Smolenskaya Naberezhnaya 10. Tel: 956 7200. www.britemb.msk.ru*
USA: *Novinskiy Bulvar 19/23. Tel: 728 5000/5577. www.usembassy.state.gov*

St Petersburg (consulates):
UK: *Proletarskoy Diktatury Ploshchad 5. Tel: 320 3200. www.britain.spb.ru*
USA: *Furshtadskaya 15. Tel: 331 2600. www.usconsulate.spb.ru*

Emergency Telephone Numbers
The following can be called free of charge in both cities from any public telephone:
Fire *01*
Police *02*
Ambulance *03*
   In the event of theft or illness, a better bet is to turn to your hotel or embassy.

Health
Your travel insurance policy should give good cover for medical treatment. Russian hospitals are grim, foreign-staffed clinics are expensive. Both cities offer well-stocked pharmacies, but travellers are advised to bring their own prescribed medications and contraceptives. No injections are mandatory before arrival, though some doctors advise diphtheria and hepatitis inoculations. AIDS is present of course.
   Moscow's tap water is allegedly safe. In St Petersburg, it is better to buy water bottles that one can find in any food shop.

   In an emergency, either speak to your embassy doctor or contact the following medical clinics or pharmacies:
Clinics
American Medical Centre, *Grokholskiy Pereulok, Moscow. Tel: 933 7700.*
St Petersburg, *Serpuhovskaya 10. Tel: 326 1730. www.amcenters.com*
Athens Medical Centre, *Michurinskiy Prospekt 6, Moscow. Tel: 147 9322.*
European Medical Centre
Moscow: *Spiridonievskiy Pereulok 5. Tel: 933 6655. www.emcmos.ru*
St Petersburg: *Suvorovskiy Prospekt 60. Tel: 327 0301. www.euromed.ru*
Mediclub Moscow, *Michurinskiy Prospekt 56. Tel: 931 5018. www.mediclub.ru*

Dental
Moscow:
European Dental Centre, *1-y Nikoloschepovskiy Pereulok 5. Tel: 933 0002. Open Mon–Fri.*
St Petersburg:
Medi chain, *Moskovskiy Prospekt 79. Tel: 324 0005. Open 24 hours.*

Pharmacies
Moscow:
Chudo Doktor, *Tverskaya 24/2. Tel: 299 5885. Open 24 hrs. Metro: Mayakovskaya/ Tversakaya/Pushkinskaya.*
Petrovskaya, *Pharmacy Petrovka 19. Tel: 923 2446.*
Stariy Lekar, *Arbat 51. Tel: 244 0021. Open 24 hrs. Metro: Smolenskaya.*
St Petersburg:
PetroFarm, *Nevskiy Prospekt 22. Tel: 314 5401. Open 24 hrs and Nevskiy Prospekt 83. Tel: 277 5962. Metro: Nevskiy Prospekt/Gostiniy Dvor.*

Doktor, *Liteyniy Prospekt 7.*
Tel: 273 6135. Open 24 hrs. Metro:
Mayakovskaya.

Before travelling always ensure you have adequate travel insurance. You can obtain up-to-date advice on health matters from Thomas Cook travel consultants.

Maps and Additional Information

The best maps of Moscow and St Petersburg are printed by Russian Information Services (*28 East State Street, Montpellier, VT 05602 USA. Tel: 802 223 4955. www.infoservices.com/moscow/*). They are included in the directories *Where in Moscow* and *Where in St Petersburg*, both widely available in Russia.

The *Traveller's Yellow Pages*, published for both cities by InfoServices International Inc (*1 Saint Mark's Place, Cold Spring Harbor, NY 11724 USA. Tel: 516 549 0064*), contain a wealth of practical information in English; obtainable in hotel lobby kiosks.

Media

Foreign newspapers are on sale in hotels and Western-style supermarkets. Several local English-language newspapers are available free, including *The Moscow Times* and the *St Petersburg Times*. The entertainments listings are invaluable.

Most hotels are equipped with CNN and satellite broadcasts. The Moscow local TV channel shows BBC news in English at 7.45am weekdays and 7.00am at weekends.

BBC radio's World Service broadcasts on 1260kHz medium wave.

Money Matters

One rouble is theoretically divided into 100 kopecks, but in practice the lowest denomination in circulation is the one rouble coin.

Do not change money on the streets since both city centres are littered with bureaux de change – *obmyen valyuty* – and private deals remain illegal. Banknotes printed before 1993 are no longer legal tender. Dollars and euros are the easiest to change, but torn or marked bills and pre-1988 dollars are often refused. Bring sterling or US dollar denomination traveller's cheques in small values. These are not as useful as credit cards, however, which can be used in ATMs located around both cities.

In case of theft, Thomas Cook MasterCard cheques can be refunded by reporting the loss on *(44) 1733 318 950* (reverse charges).

Credit cards are generally accepted in foreign-run shops, hotels, larger restaurants and travel agents. Some banks offer cash advances on Visa and MasterCard. In case of theft, phone Moscow *(095) 933 6636 (Amex)*, *956 4806 (Mastercard, Visa, Diners Club)*. American Express is based in Moscow at *Usacheva 3* (*tel: 933 6636*) and in St Petersburg in *Malaya Morskaya Ul 23* (*tel: 326 4500*).

Maps, newspapers and magazines may be bought at numerous newspaper stands

LANGUAGE

Pronunciation

With a few exceptions, Russian words are pronounced the way they are read. Knowing which syllable to stress, however, takes experience. Just speak slowly and hope for the best.

А/а – ah in 'bar'

Б/б – b

В/в – v

Г/г – g except in words like Грозного when it is pronounced as a v

Д/д – d

Е/е – yeh in 'yes'

Ё/ё – yoh in 'yoghurt'

Ж/ж – zh in 'treasure'

З/з – z

И/и – ee in 'Eden'

Й/Й – softer than the above, like the y in 'joy'

К/к – k

Л/л – l

М/м – m

Н/н – n

О/о – oh in 'fort' when stressed, otherwise ah in 'bar'

П/п – p

Р/р – r, rolled like an Italian r

С/с – s

Т/т – t

У/у – oo in 'school'

Ф/ф – f

Х/х – kh in the Scottish 'loch'

Ц/ц – ts in 'pretzel'

Ч/ч – ch in 'church'

Ш/ш – sh in 'shoe'

Щ/щ – shch in 'fresh cheese'

Ы/ы – i in 'ilk' but more guttural

Э/э – e in 'end'

Ю/ю – yoo in 'universe'

Я/я – ya in 'yard'

Ь, Ъ – soft sign and hard sign – both affect preceding consonant

Basic words and phrases

yes – da – ДА

no – nyet – НЕТ

please – pazhalsta – ПОЖАЛУЙСТА

thank you – spaseeba – СПАСИБО

excuse me/I'm sorry – izvineetyeh – ИЗВИНИТЕ

good morning – dobroye ootra – ДОБРОЕ УТРО

good afternoon – dobry dyen – ДОБРЫЙ ДЕНЬ

good evening – dobry vyecher – ДОБРЫЙ ВЕЧЕР

good night – spakoiny nochi – СПОКОЙНОЙ НОЧИ

I have... – oo menya... – У МЕНЯ…

I haven't... – oo menya nyet... – У МЕНЯ НЕТ…

Do you speak English? – Vwi gavareetyeh pa angleesky? – ВЫ ГОВОРИТЕ ПО АНГЛИЙСКИЙ?

I do not understand – Yah nye panimahyoo – Я НЕ ПОНИМАЮ

Repeat it, please – Pavtareetyeh pazhalsta – ПОВТОРИТЕ ПОЖАЛУЙСТА

May I?/Do you mind? – Mozhna? – МОЖНО?]

How much does... cost? – Skolka stoyit...? – СКОЛЬКО СТОИТ…?

when – kagdah – КОГДА

yesterday – vcherah – ВЧЕРА

today – sevodnyah – СЕГОДНЯ

tomorrow – zavtra – ЗАВТРА

at what time...? – vah skolka...? – ВО СКОЛЬКО…?

where is...? – gdyeh...? – ГДЕ…?

here – zdyes – ЗДЕСЬ
there – tam – ТАМ
near – *bleez*ka – БЛИЗКО
far – dale*koh* – ДАЛЕКО
behind – zah – ЗА
opposite – na *protiv* – НАПРОТИВ
in front of – pye*red* – ПЕРЕД
to the right – na *prava* – НА ПРАВО
to the left – na *lyeva* – НА ЛЕВО
straight on – vper*yod* – ВПЕРЁД
street – *ool*itsa – УЛИЦА
petrol station – benzaka*lonka* –
   БЕНЗОКОЛОНКА
airport – ayero*port* – АЭРОПОРТ
railway station – vok*zal* – ВОКЗАЛ
platform – plat*forma* –
   ПЛАТФОРМА
bus stop – asta*novka* –
   ОСТАНОВКА
metro station – *stah*ntsia me*troh* –
   СТАНЦИЯ МЕТРО
price – tse*na* – ЦЕНА
ticket office – *ka*ssa – КАССА
ticket – bil*yet* – БИЛЕТ

Quantity
one – a*deen* – ОДИН
two – dva – ДВА
three – tree – ТРИ
four – che*teeri* – ЧЕТЫРЕ
five – pyat – ПЯТЬ
six – shyest – ШЕСТЬ
seven – syem – СЕМЬ
eight – *vohsyem* – ВОСЕМЬ
nine – *dyev*yat – ДЕВЯТЬ
10 – *dyes*yat – ДЕСЯТЬ
100 – stoh – СТО
1,000 – *tees*yacha – ТИСЯЧА
a little – nye*mnoh*ga – НЕМНОГО
enough – *khva*htit – ХВАТИТ
many/much – *mnoh*ga – МНОГО

too many/too much – *sleesh*kom
   *mnoh*ga – СЛИШКОМ МНОГО

Days and months
Monday – pani*dyel*nik –
   ПОНЕДЕЛЬНИК
Tuesday – *vtor*nik – ВТОРНИК
Wednesday – srye*dah* – СРЕДА
Thursday – *chet*vyehrg – ЧЕТВЕРГ
Friday – *pyat*nitsa – ПЯТНИЦА
Saturday – soo*boh*ta – СУББОТА
Sunday – voskr*esen*yeh –
   ВОСКРЕСЕНЬЕ
January – yan*var* – ЯНВАРЬ
February – fev*ral* – ФЕВРАЛЬ
March – mart – МАРТ
April – ap*ryel* – АПРЕЛЬ
May – mai – МАЙ
June – i*yoon* – ИЮНЬ
July – i*yool* – ИЮЛЬ
August – ahv*goost* – АВТУСТ
September – sent*yah*br –
   СЕНТЯБРЬ
October – ak*tya*br – ОКТЯБРЬ
November – nay*abr* – НОЯБРЬ
December – dek*abr* – ДЕКАБРЬ]

Large, air-conditioned shopping centres are not
uncommon anymore

Opening Hours

Shops open Monday to Saturday 9am–6 or 7pm. Larger stores stay open until 8pm, and many of them, including foreign-run supermarkets, trade on Sundays. Many kiosks, especially around railway stations, are open 24 hours a day.

Photography

Military bases and the like remain off limits, and militia officers may object if you point a lens directly at them (if so, take note). Otherwise you are unlikely to encounter problems.

Film, including Polaroid cartridges, is widely available, but any video cassettes other than VHS format should be brought from home. Express developing and printing points are easy to find in both cities. Try **Servistsentr** in Moscow (*Ulitsa Novy Arbat 17*) or **Agfa** in St Petersburg (*Lermontovskiy Pr 50, Tel: 251 0519*).

PLACES OF WORSHIP
Moscow:

Catholic Chaplaincy: *Kutuzovskiy Prospekt 7/4. Sat 6pm (English and French), Sun 6pm (English). Tel: 243 9621.* Protestant Chaplaincy: *Voznesenskiy Pereulok 8. Sun services at 10am, 11.30am and 3pm at St Andrew's Church. www.moscowprotestantchaplaincy.org* Synagogue: *Arkhipova Ulitsa 14. Tel: 923 9697.* Mosque: *Vypolzov Pereulok 7. Tel: 281 3866.*

St Petersburg:

Lutheran Church of St Peter, *Nevskiy Pr 22–4. Tel: 312 0798.* Mosque: *Kronverkskiy Prospekt 7. Tel: 233 9819.*

Roman Catholic Church of St Catherine, *Nevskiy Pr 32–4. Tel: 311 5795/7170.* Synagogue: *Lermonovskiy Prospekt 2 (behind the Mariinskiy Theatre). No phone.*

Post

Stamps, postcards and envelopes can be bought in most hotels, but the Russian postal service is best not relied upon for important letters and packages.

The following international courier agencies operate out of both cities: **DHL** *Tel: 941 8417.* (Moscow). *www.dhl.ru* **TNT** *Tel: 797 2777* (Moscow); *tel: 718 3330* (St Petersburg). *www.tnt.ru* **Federal Express** *Tel: 787 555* (Moscow); *tel: 325 8825* (St Petersburg). *www.fedex.com* **UPS** *Tel: 961 2211* (Moscow); *tel: 327 8540* (St Petersburg). *www.ups.com*

PUBLIC TRANSPORT
Metro

The metro systems are cheap, clean, efficient and safe even at night. A grasp of the Cyrillic alphabet is essential to making sense of the signs.

A neon letter M (red in Moscow, blue in St Petersburg) indicates a station entrance. ВХОД (*vkhod*) on the swing doors means entrance, ВЫХОД (*vykhod*) exit. Tokens (*zhetoni*) are on sale at the *kassa* (cash desk), but a modest outlay will buy a monthly season ticket (*prisnoy bilet*, on sale till the 8th of each month) either for the metro alone (*proezdnoy*) or overground transport as well (*yedeeni bilyet*). Signs overhead and on the walls indicate which platform to wait at.

On the train, you are expected to give up your seat to old people and women with children. On arrival, a recorded voice announces the station and the connections. To get out, head for the ВЫХОД В ГОРОД (*vykhod v gorod*) sign. If there is more than one exit, the sign says which takes you where. To change lines, look for ПЕРЕХОД (*perekhod*) – meaning crossing – indicated by a figure walking up steps on a blue background.

The metro in both cities opens before 6am and last changes must be made by 1am in Moscow and 11.30pm in St Petersburg. The metro map for Moscow is on *pp24–5* and for St Petersburg on *pp28–9*.

Buses, Trams and Trolleybuses

To make full use of the overground networks requires a high degree of insider knowledge. Tickets valid for all three are sold in strips of ten and can be bought from the drivers. You punch them yourself in the contraptions inside the vehicle. *See also p28.*

Suburban Trains

Many sights outside the city are best reached by the suburban trains, known as *elektrichka*. Tickets, bought at the railway station from the *prigorodny kassi* (often located in a separate part of the station), are very cheap. On the platform, the train will be identified by its final destination which you should check on the diagram in the ticket hall. Not every train stops at each station, so check with fellow passengers before boarding.

Taxis

Stopping a taxi (*taksi*) is simple,

especially in the centre of town – hold your arm out and a queue of eager drivers will soon pull up. Official taxis (marked by a 'T' in a circle) are equipped with meters, but raging inflation made them obsolete. The fare should be agreed before you get in (bear in mind that fares are rapidly approaching world levels). If necessary, write down the fare and the destination.

Many 'taxis' are simply private cars or government vehicles whose drivers are earning a little on the side. They are cheaper, but a degree of caution is advisable. Never get in a car which already has passengers and do not let the driver pick up additional fares on the way. Women travelling alone at night should avoid taxis completely.

Taxis can be booked from your hotel or by telephone: in Moscow, call *927 0000* or *928 6868*; in St Petersburg, call *312 0022*. Allow at least an hour. Many Western-run hotels have their own taxis which are far superior to the local service but much pricier.

Travelling between Moscow and St Petersburg

The easiest and cheapest method is by overnight train, leaving either city around midnight and arriving around 8 or 9am. The 'Intourist' and 'Krasnaya Strela' services are the most comfortable. Many hotels will arrange your journey for you, but independent travellers should come with their passport to the station to buy a ticket in advance. For details and timetables for trains running between Moscow and St Petersburg consult the Thomas Cook European Timetable, which is available to buy online at *www.thomascookpublishing.com*, from Thomas Cook branches in the UK or by calling *01733 416477*.

In Moscow, Leningradskiy Vokzal (Leningrad Station) is at *Komsomolskaya Ploshchad 3 (metro: Komsomolskaya)*. In St Petersburg, Moskovskiy Vokzal (Moscow Station) is at *Nevskiy Prospekt 85 (metro: Ploshchad Vosstaniya), tel: 168 4044*. Train information: (Moscow) *Tel: 266 9000/9333*. (St Petersburg) *Tel: 168 0111*.
American Express Moscow, *Sadovaya Kudrinskaya. Tel: 755 9000*.
American Express St Petersburg, *Grand Hotel Europe Mikhailovsaya Shosse 1/7. Tel: 329 6060*.
Central Railway Agency, *Komsomolskaya Ploshchad 5. Tel: 266 8333*.
Infinity Travel, *Tel: 234 6555. www.infinity.ru*
NB: See **Crime** (*p180*).

Sustainable Tourism

Thomas Cook is a strong advocate of ethical and fairly traded tourism and believes that the travel experience should be as good for the places visited as it is for the people who visit them. That's why we firmly support The Travel Foundation: a charity that develops solutions to help improve and protect holiday destinations, their environment, traditions and culture. To find out what you can do to make a positive difference to the places you travel to and the people who live there, please visit *www.thetravelfoundation.org.uk*

Telephones

Public phone boxes taking phone cards have largely replaced the old pay phones using tokens. In Moscow, look out for blue MTTS booths in metro stations and other public places – instructions are available in English at the press of a button. In St Petersburg, the SPT phone booths are green and white. Phone cards are on sale in metro stations, post offices and some banks. Phone cards can be used for local, intercity and international calls.

For an intercity call on local lines, dial 8 and wait for the tone. The code for Moscow is 095, for St Petersburg 812. The country code for Russia is 7.

To call internationally, dial 8, wait for the tone, dial 10 and the country code:
Australia *61* **Canada and USA** *1*
New Zealand *64* **UK** *44*
Then dial the full number.

Faxes can be sent from large hotels and business centres (*see the list on pp176–7*). The Central Telegraph Office in Moscow is at *Tverskaya 7 (Tel: 924 9004. Open: daily 8am–10pm)*, the Main Post Office is at *Myasnitskaya 26/2 (Tel: 924 6600. Open: Mon–Fri 8am–8pm, Sat 8am–7pm & Sun 9am–7pm)*; in St Petersburg, the Main Post Office is at *Pochtamtskaya 9 (Tel: 312 8302. Open: Mon–Sat 9am–7.30pm, Sun 10am–5.30pm)*.

See also **On Business** *pp176–7*.

Time

Both cities run three hours ahead of GMT, eight hours ahead of New York time. Summer time, when clocks go forward an hour, begins on the last Saturday of March and ends on the last Saturday of October.

Tipping

With the exception of taxi drivers, who invariably charge double for foreigners, tip as you would anywhere else.

Toilets

Russian public toilets are rare and awful. Go out armed with paper and use restaurant or museum facilities.

Tourist Information

There is no Tourist Information Office in Moscow so visitors should use the service bureaus in large hotels. St Petersburg is better served. The City Tourist Information Centres are at *Dvortsovaya Ploshchad 12 (Palace Square)* and *Sadovaya 14/52. Tel: 310 2822. www.ctic.spb.ru. Open Mon–Fri 10am–7pm, Sat 10am–6pm, Sun (summer only) 10am–6pm.*

Tours in the Cities

Moscow's best group, 'Patriarshiy Dom' (*tel: 795 0927*), runs guided tours in English, including a purpose-built Moscow orientation trip and walking tours. In St Petersburg, ask at the City Information Centre (*tel: 310 2822. www.ctic.spb.ru*).

TRAVEL AGENCIES

A number of companies take telephone bookings for internal and international flights. Some book hotels and car hire.

Moscow:

Air Tour, *Leningradskoe Shosse 80, floor 2. Tel: 451 8230/105 3030. www.aerotour.ru*

Barry Martin Travel, *Malaya Kommunisticheskaya Ulitsa 3/9 Building 1. Tel: 911 9242.*

Grifon Travel, *Hotel Ukraine room 743. Tel: 243 2595.*

IntelService Center, *Leninskiy Prospekt 29 suites 401–8. Tel: 956 4422. www.intelservice.ru*

Intourist, *Milyutinskiy Pereulok 13/1. Tel: 956 8844. Also at Mokhovaya 13. Tel: 292 2260.*

Time Travel, *Ulitsa Pistsovaya 12. Tel: 257 9220.*

St Petersburg:

East West Kontaktservice, *Nevskiy Prospekt 105. Tel: 327 3416/272 8761; fax: 327 3417. www.ostwest.com*

MIR, *Nevskiy Pr 11. Tel: 325 7122. www.mirtc.ru*

Russkiye Kruizy, *Nevskiy Pr 51. Tel: 325 6120/1150. www.russian-cruises.ru*

Cosmos Ltd, *2nd line of Vasilevskiy Island 35. Tel: 327 7256.*

Travellers with Disabilities

Russia offers little help for travellers with disabilities. Access to the metro and other forms of public transport is all but ruled out, and few buildings have ramps. However, Russians often go out of their way to lend a hand in a tricky moment.

Access Travel, *6 The Hillock, Astley, Lancs M29 7GW. Tel: 01942 888844. www.access-travel.co.uk*

Mobility International (*www.miusa.org*) may be able to assist with enquiries.

Society for the Advancement of Travelers with Handicaps (SATH), *347 5th Avenue, New York, NY 10016. Tel: 212 447 7284. www.sath.org*

Women Travellers

Most Western-type supermarkets and pharmacies stock sanitary products.

Russian men may seem chauvinistic but do not intend to offend. However, if you feel sexually harassed, cause a public scene rather than ignore it. At night, keep off backstreets and avoid lone taxi rides. 'Mace' spray canisters are legal in Russia.

ACKNOWLEDGEMENTS

Thomas Cook Publishing wishes to thank DEMETRIO CARRASCO for the photographs reproduced in this book, to whom the copyright in the photographs belong, with the exception of the following:

JON ARNOLD: pages 9, 14, 15, 16, 27b, 33, 34a, 34b, 37, 39, 44, 48, 50, 56, 59, 63, 80–81, 85, 87, 98, 119, 134, 141, 142, 144a, 160, 162b, 170, 171, 175a, 175b, 176

KEN PATERSON: 5, 18b, 20a, 23b, 35, 48a, 49, 51, 53, 71, 88, 99, 129, 130, 135a, 135b, 140b, 158, 172a, 172b, 174, 179

Copy-editing: GERARD HILL

Index: INDEXING SPECIALISTS (UK) LTD

Maps: UPDATED BY RICHARD MORRIS

Proof-reading: JAN McCANN for CAMBRIDGE PUBLISHING MANAGEMENT LTD

Send your thoughts to
books@thomascook.com

We're committed to providing the very best up-to-date information in our travel guides and constantly strive to make them as useful as they can be. You can help us to improve future editions by letting us have your feedback. If you've made a wonderful discovery on your travels that we don't already feature, if you'd like to inform us about recent changes to anything that we do include, or if you simply want to let us know your thoughts about this guidebook and how we can make it even better – we'd love to hear from you.

Send us ideas, discoveries and recommendations today and then look out for your valuable input in the next edition of this title. And, as an extra 'thank you' from Thomas Cook Publishing, you'll be automatically entered into our exciting monthly prize draw.

Emails to the above address, or letters to Travellers Project Editor, Thomas Cook Publishing, PO Box 227, Units 15–16, Coningsby Road, Peterborough PE3 8SB, UK.

Please don't forget to let us know which title your feedback refers to!